An Episodic Interpretation of the Mahabharata

R.N. SARKAR

ATLANTIC PUBLISHERS & DISTRIBUTORS
4215/1, Ansari Road, Darya Ganj
New Delhi-110002

Published by
Atlantic Publishers & Distributors,
4215/1, Ansari Road, Darya Ganj,
New Delhi-110002

Head Office :
B-2, Vishal Enclave, Najafgarh Road,
New Delhi-110027
Phone : 5413460

Printed at : Devendra Printers through Chawla Composers,
New Delhi

FOREWORD

I have known Dr. R.N. Sarkar for some time through his contributions to *Hinduism* of London over the years. His articles on the Indo-European link of languages and literature in this journal have greatly impressed me and some European scholars. From a portion of his article on the Mahabharata published in this magazine I have a very high idea of his style and equipment, sufficient to probe rightly the heart of the many outstanding Indian myths which he deals with in this book. In our journal by his standard of scholarly inquiries into different issues of Indian literature of the mythical age he belongs with men like G. Feuerstein, M. Litt., F.R.A.I. (Durham University), Dr. Ruth Reyna, M.A., Ph.D., Swami Tathagatananda, Ian K. Watson and A. Holmes. I hope this book on the Mahabharata would acquaint the West with many half-forgotten gems of the East.

Sd. SWAMI PURNANADA
EDITOR
Hinduism (A Bi-monthly Journal)
17, Stanlake Villas,
London, W-12

FOREWORD

It was known to Dr. [illegible] for some time through his contributions to *Hinduism* of London [illegible] the [illegible] link of the [illegible] and literature [illegible] journal [illegible] and some European scholars. From [illegible] article on the Mahabharata published in this magazine I [illegible] a very [illegible] of his style and [illegible] suffice it to [illegible] the [illegible] Indian myths which he deals with in this book [illegible] its standard [illegible] inquiries into [illegible] literature [illegible] He belongs with [illegible] like G[illegible] M[illegible] (Durham University) [illegible] P[illegible] M.A., [illegible] I [illegible] this book on the Mahabharata would [illegible] the West [illegible] many half forgotten gems of the East.

A. Swami P[illegible]
Editor
Hinduism (A [illegible] Monthly Journal)
17, Stan[illegible] Villas,
London W-1[illegible]

PREFACE

The plan of the book was long in hibernation, some articles based on different episodes of Indian epics were published in different Organs of Satsang, some published from Deoghar, some from Calcutta, and some from Bangladesh, all in Bengali. None of the articles of course is included in the present work. All those only served as a healthy impulse to a systematic study of some other interesting episodes of the epic which has been accepted as the greatest epic, not only of the East, but also of the whole world. The final encouragement came, of course, from Swami Purnananda, Editor of the *Hinduism* (London), who asked me to write on his own plan something for his Magazine, particularly detailing the significance of the Oriental contribution to the Occidental heritage of language and culture, just upon publication in it of a part of one of the articles now arranged under the title. I have not, however, attempted in the present volume any comparative evaluation of the epics of the East and the West, I have only tried to assess the timeless truths concealed in the mythical apparatus of the epic through explication of a limited number of its episodes in close touch with the original Sanskrit texts, often quoted in Roman script.

I have not really written a separate article on the special character of the epic style and method of presentation which is a part of the truth itself when shorn of its exotic expletives. But I have here and there pointed out the peculiarities of the style and their close bearings upon the hidden substance. I have also kept as much closer to the evolution of the story in every episode as may serve as an extra attraction even to those who are least interested in its literary achievement, although ever taking particular care not to blur the literary excellence of the author's treatment, an author who is still famed as one of the greatest poets the world has produced. The treatment in these pages, however, is not of the Daniken type, nor of the Columbia University Press publication type, nor of any other known or unknown system of presentment, readers must see it.

In my labour I have been encouraged by some of my old and present friends, and some of my best teachers, of them I name first Dr. Ramaranjan Mukherji, ex-Vice Chancellor of Rabindra Bharati and Burdwan University, Dr. Kshudiram Das, ex-Ramtanu Lahiri Professor, Calcutta University, and Prafulla Kumar Das, ex-Vice Principal, Manomohini Institute of Technology and ex-Editor, *Alochana* (Satsang).

Particular mention is due to Swami Purnananda who has kindly written a word of introduction to this book at my request, and to Professor Joykali Bhattacharya who has gone through the Sanskrit texts in this book for revision.

The text I use is from the North Indian edition of the Mahabharata (Gita Press) supplemented by the South Indian edition wherever necessary and for textual interpretation I have constantly referred to Monier Williams and Macdonell who chaired at different times Boden Professorship at Oxford and done away with all diacritical marks in all English transcriptions of original Sanskrit for universal intelligibility.

R.N. SARKAR

CONTENTS

KRISHNA'S VISWARUPA AT THE KAURAVA COURT

The Lord's all-pervasive omnipresence, called Viswarupa, was shown to Arjuna in the battlefield, this was also shown to many others including Dhritarastra in the Assembly Hall of the latter when he came there on a mission of truce; how was it possible and how did it come, the present article seeks to inquire into this side of the subject.

(1)

Lord Krishna himself came to make the last attempt of truce between the warring families of kinsmen. He reached the court of Dhritarastra where he was received by all with due civilities. The text of the Mahabharata reveals he must have been accompanied by Rishi Narada, who was sent there as an unfailing feeler before direct negotiation could be initiated. Narada first met Dhritarastra personally to tell him the purpose of Lord Krishna's mission. Dhritarastra thereupon pleaded his helplessness with his son Duryadhana :

Bhagabannebamebaitad yathā badasi Nārada,
Ichchhāmi chāhamapyebang na tvīsho Bhagabannaham.

(Yudyog Parba, Chap. 134, 1.)

The king himself took the initiative to approach Krishna, the honoured guest at his court; he perhaps thought it meet to explain to him his very precarious position in the palace. He told him all that he had suggested were quite right and according to the stipulations of Dharma, and nothing could be more conducive to the interest of life and the world; but Krishna must know that things were not as he wished, his sons were not within the pale of his authority; he should seek his Lordship's help to teach Duryadhana sense and to avert that repugnant act of irreligion. He narrated also how of late that son of his had grown too impertinent to listen to the advice and good counsel of his well-meaning mentors, his own mother Gandhari, and men like Bhishma and Vidura. He doggedly defied the tutelage of the greybeards. Upon all these cofidences made to him Dhritarastra entreated Lord Krishna to personally intervene to restrain that vile creature Duryadhana :

Anushādhi durātmānang svayang Duryodhanang Nripam,
Suhritkāryang tu sumahat kritang te syajjanārdana.

(Ibid. 6-7)

At this humble submission of Dhritarastra Krishna turned to reach Duryadhana. He first drew his attention to his noble birth and his natural endowments, and then quietly held up the justness of truce, and also pointed out how wrong would be his determined stance of intransigence, which only goes with the low-born, cruel and the brazen sort. He held out to him the prospect of conciliation and also the horror of war, and told him that his choice of war-path would not only be a threat to his own existence but also to all his accomplices and proteges. Lord Krishna moreover attributed to him all the good qualities he should have possessed, being born of a rare ancient family of established renown. He recounted, too, some personal excellences of the very inspiring kind and expected he should willingly obey his guardians and keep the world free from the bane of war. Then he gave him his reading of others' minds, all his ministers, friends, generals and parents wanted conciliation with the Pandava brothers. It now rests on you to give effect to their silent desire, Krishna said. In this way Lord Krishna threw a feeler and waited for Duryadhana's reaction.

By way of exposition Lord Krishna presented to him both the sides of the picture, war and peace; he had rather gone into a thorough discourse on the ethical values of life that might concern this present case. Eventually he ended up by explaining the full implication of the stance of virtue and his personal patronage of the side where it lay. Even war with the highest might on their side against the seemingly weak armed with virtue would not avail, virtue will triumph in the long run. So peace would finally protect his interest, the Pandavas would surely crown his father supreme monarch and elect him Crown Prince.

Lord Krishna's exhortation inspired similar outlook in Duryadhana's best generals like Bhisma and Drona. It was not immediately known what Duryadhana's reaction was, because before he could say anything Bhisma took the cue from Krishna's peroration to admonish him. He advised him to act upon Krishna's good lesson, he thought none could achieve any good either for himself or for others by simply disoblizing him. It was time for him to mend his ways and fall upon the wishes of the Lord. Drona took this opportunity to offer his views. He asked Duryadhana to listen to Bhisma's words and Krishna's advice. No good would he derive out of his impertinent act. It would be absolutely against his own interest to disobey Krishna in a fit of blinding insolence. The people who had instigated him would not in the time of crisis be by his side, he warned. Then Vidura came to proclaim his view of peace. He became a little more harsh in his reproach; he was perhaps extremely annoyed at the haughty nature of Duryadhana, he was sure he was all too steeped in sin for correction, and had no wish to offer him good counsel. But he was really very sorry for the parents who had brought him as a curse to the whole family and the world, they must lose all their friends and kin for that great enemy of a son and would have to beg for their living on earth quite deprived of all resources.

When a pious man like Vidura spoke thus anticipating the future consequence of Duryadhana's intransigence, Dhritarastra just broke in to make an appeal to his son's good sense, whom he may have suspected already firm on his design. He asked him to accept Krishna's proposal of truce, because he knew none could prosper scorning Krishna's wisdom, victory would be simply an illusion without Dharma that Krishna taught men to practise in life. He was sure the Pandavas were on the path of virtue under the direct guardianship of the all-knowing Lord Krishna, and all his assurance of peace would do Duryadhana immense good and crown him with success in life and give the peace of mind which he most needed. He must not spurn Krishna's good mission and bring about total disaster.

At this stage both the generals Bhisma and Drona spoke in one voice warning Duryadhana against the grim prospect of war. They asked him to consider before the Pandava brothers were in full trim of war-preparation. He should think they were still not in mind to fight. They depicted for Duryadhana that scene of horror if once Arjuna, Bhima and Yudhisthira with full support of Krishna went into fighting.

This is only a bare skeleton of how they took Krishna's mission, how all of them wanted to avoid war and seriously considered the Lord's role of an emissary. But all their appeals, entreaties, and rebuffs made practically no impression on Duryadhana's mind. His reaction was not only unhelpful but quite hostile and comminatory. He tried to exculpate himself from the charge of wrongs. He pretended to have followed the stipulated principle of a true Kshatriya.

He accused even Lord Krishna of his partisan and dubious role. Along with his war-preceptor, grandfather and father, Krishna made it a point to find fault with him, leaving alone all other rulers of the earth. But he saw no reason to be so admonished by them, nor any sufficient reason for the unqualified glorification of the Pandavas either. They were defeated in a game of dice by Sakuni, where practically he had no part to play. They lost their stake in it, which again was not forced on them. Krishna's mission seemed to him a covert threat, but a true Kshatriya should not be so bullied. If they had thrown down the gauntlet it was no wrong to pick it up. He then went to the extreme length of challenging Krishna's authority to plead for peace when he had already sided with the Pandavas. Surely he had better court death in the battlefield than turn his back to the swords of his enemies. He would allow the Pandavas to share not even a particle of earth that the point of a needle may prick without war. Quite evident that the fate is decided.

Duryadhana was full of arrongance and every word he uttered was charged with it. Even a bare account which is attempted above may bear it out. Duryadhana was surely blind with pride and rage, both are blinding enough. He could fault Krishna because of utter stupefaction of reason under their obsessive force. His interpretation of Dharma and the ethics of the Kshatriya cult was a dazed interpretation of obsession. Lord Krishna knew it, so his first reaction to Duryadhana's muffled accusation was a subdued simper half playing upon his lips. Then he did exactly what the occasion demanded. A kind of shock-treatment is the only answer to obsession-ridden nerves, to bring them back to composure out of their physical distortion. Lord Krishna struck in a rude piece of warning :

Lapsyase bīrashayanang kāmametadabāpsasi

[Ibid. Chap. 128, 2]

You will have a hero's death as you wish, I tell you.

When Krishna told this he administered a shock and also disclosed a truth; Duryadhana took neither. He was all too galvanized into the spirit of conflict for that. Although Krishna knew any amount of explication or elaboration of the case would simply pass over his dull head, yet something by way of analysis, he thought, should be said for others' ears at least. He took up the contention of Duryadhana's just treatment of the Pandavas. He drew the attention of the other rulers of the earth; Duryadhana alleged he did play no part in that game of dice in which the Pandavas lost their all, but who did not know that he played a part from behind the curtain and Sakuni was only his instrument ? It was secretly planned by him, now hypocritically to pretend innocence was the gravest of sins. No doubt it was due to his envy of the Pandava brothers' rightly deserved prosperity. Then Krishna went on analysing one after another all Duryadhana's insidious acts. 'It is known to all that the game of dice is tricky enough for the plain-hearted to be outwitted by the crooked-minded who take it easy to gain in divisive purposes and material distress,' Krishna told them. 'You have caused this great distress to them through the game of dice, who although themselves on the path of virtue got mixed up with the evil doers without knowing the effect.' He asked, 'who could haul down to the open court a brother's wife but you ? You have dragged Droupadi, the beloved wife of the Pandava brothers, and by nature bashful and full of womanly grace, up there into the presence of the courtiers to expose her savagely to ridicule.'

Lord Krishna recounted one by one all Duryadhana's misdeeds. He grudged them not only their father's just share of the kingdom but their life as well. He disclosed all his concealed foul plays, and the caucus of misalliance of the three—Karna, Sakuni and Dushasana. And finally he warned that he was going to ignore the sincerest appeal of his parents and guardians Bhisma, Drona and Vidura not for his good but to meet the sad end of his life and wealth; he was pursuing the path of evil and engaging in inglorious feats.

Never does the Lord do anything out of personal grudge, all his acts and tricks are prompted by the highest care for the good of all, he is all good as he is all-powerful. Even the scalding reprimand that he had resorted to had one ulterior motive and it was partly realized : all the generals of Duryadhana could see the truth of the case which they could not with an obsessed vision; and Dushasana, one of the henchmen, and his own brother, was now out of his craze for power, definitely under the impact of Krishna's soul-searching expose. Dushasana broke in to draw his brother's attention to the seamy side of the case, and only half-pronounced his views leaving out all inessential exordium : 'Oh King, if you do not make peace with the Pandavas at your own will the Kauravas will place you under arrest and deliver to the sons of Kunti. Even father, Bhisma and Drona will soon leave us three—you, Karna and myself—into the clutches of the Pandavas.'

Na chet sangdhāsyase rājan svena kāmena Pāndabaih,
Badhvā kilatvāng dāsyanti Kuntīputrāya Kaurabāh.
Baikartanang tvang cha māng cha trīnetāng manujarsabha,
Pāndabebhyah prasādanti Bhismo Drānah pito cha te.

(Ibid. 23-24)

So long Duryadhana sat there altogether grumpy and sullen in the full court of assembled dignitaries. Now when his own brother expressed his view against him and against war he rose at his seat and arrongantly and discourteously to the august presence of Bhisma, Drona, Somadatta, Vidura, Dhritarastra and Janardana himself prepared to withdraw accompanied by his brothers.

When Duryadhana was thus withdrawing with all insolence of manners Bhisma repeated once more his timely warning for the ears of the assembled Kshatriya rulers : The man who abjures the path of Dharma will soon come to grief even to the ridicule of the enemies. This wicked-hearted prince, the son of Dhritarastra, not knowing true manners, haughty and slave to his passions will surely fall like a ripe fruit with all his allies of earth rulers.

(3)

Lord Krishna understood that except a few led by Duryadhana none wanted war, even the celebrated generals of the Kaurava army wanted peace. He then suggested a lesser evil to ward off a greater massacre. He drew attention of the assembly to the two cardinal precedents to enlighten them about the methods. He referred to his own case, his dealings with Kamsa who embroiled the whole kin in cruel killings. He killed him in war only to save the whole line from total annihilation. He turned next to the episode of war between gods and demons. When they were locked in a terrible war which could have brought all life to an ineluctable end, sparing neither of the embattled sides, it made the Prime Progenitor think out a saving stroke. He cannot see the Creation finally obliterated from the scheme of existence. He summoned Dharma, that supremely well-intentioned Progenitor of all life did it, and enjoined a duty that he should arrest the unruly of the two, the Demons, the scions of Diti, and leave them in the custody of Varuna. Dharma did it and Varuna kept them constantly in the waves of the ocean.

On the strength of these illuminating instances Krishna prescribed the solution that they should likewise put the four under arrest, Duryadhana, Karna, Dushasana and Sakuni the son of Subala, and give them into the custody of the Pandavas to avert this impending crisis :

Tathā Duryodhanang Karnang Shakuning chāpi Soubalam,
Badhvā Dunshāsanang chāpi Pāndabebhyah prayachchhatha.

(Ibid. 48.)

So saying Lord Krishna outlined the principle in support of his specific edict in addition to the concrete instances.

The whole house was convinced in the way of action suggested by Lord Krishna. The man who was closest concerned, Dhritarastra, the father of the two wildly behaved sons, took the first step to act upon Krishna's advice. He called upon Vidura the most well-meaning of his ministers and asked him to bring there the pious queen Gandhari to see if she could prevail upon her impertinent sons by her very strong pleadings. Dhritarastra then told Gandhari how arrogant her son was to scorn and spurn all Krishna's good advice. Gandhari knew already what was going to happen. She explained how unjustly the old king was being carried in everything by his son's unscrupulous wishes. Duryadhana, she thought, was absolutely unworthy of the high responsibility of a ruler. When that sacred duty was reposed on an unsteady sinful and perverted head the old king must have a bitter taste of its consequences. She knew well no persuasion would change Duryadhana's mind and ways, he was already all too steeped in sins for that.

We know Duryadhana insolently left the assembly hall. So once again Vidura was sent to him to say that his mother wanted his presence there. Unwillingly as a scotched serpent he came down to the open court and impatiently sat there breathing heavily for an excuse to leave the place. Gandhari broke into a long exhortation which was practically delivered over an ill-advised drooping head. The essence of her elaborate discourse was Dharma which her son abandoned in his pursuit of the lures of passion and power. Duryadhana disqualified himself for the high responsibility of a ruler by lapsing into vice. He should, therefore, listen to Lord Krishna and make peace with the virtuous Pandava brothers.

Gandhari's long exhortation to Duryadhana bore no fruit. He left the court the soonest she ended her pleadings to meet his accomplices in secret aside. Karna, Sakuni and Dushasana were waiting for him.

(4)

Duryadhana put a wrong construction on the entire proceedings of the council chamber. He viewed Krishna's mission as thoroughly motivated and directed against him, to really build up a stronghold with Bhisma, Drona and even Dhritarastra, his own father, against his interest. The pivot of these political machinations, he thought, was Krishna himself. So he proposed to his associates that Krishna should be taken prisoner there to demoralize the whole enemy legion.

This secret conspiracy was somehow overheard by Satyaki who perhaps was well-expert in espionage. Some people must have gone round trying to ascertain the true motive of the wicked caucus. Satyaki, as soon as he smelt something wrong, took some precautionary measure : he asked one of the company commanders, Kritabarma, to alert the troops under his command and keep himself in fighting trim mounting guard at the entrance gate of the Assembly hall. He would then leave him for Lord Krishna who had to be taken into his knowledge of the secret plot. When Satyaki had already delivered his message in secret to Krishna still seated in the council hall, he turned to Dhritarastra and Vidura to tell them how a plot was going on for his arrest, of course he did it with the elaborate commentary called for on the issue. Finally he struck the essential note as to the divine role of Lord Krishna. He let them know that Lord Krishna was Purushottama, Fulfiller the best, even in his human incarnation, so he would never deviate from Dharma, the true principle of life, and could never do any evil.

Dhritarastra must have said something in his agonised mood of reproach at this stage, but Lord Krishna already took the opportunity to ventilate his own feeling and herhaps set the stage for others to realise his quintessential ubiquity (Viswarupa). He drew the old king's attention to the seamy side of the issue of his forced detention planned by his wicked son. The king must know what it would come to. If Dhritarastra wanted it Krishna might fight them or they might war against him, and the whole world knew it that he alone could face their combined assault and crush it root and branch. But Lord Krishna told the king that he would not do it, he could not adopt any sinful reprehensible course in any case. The king's sons would really harm their own interest by the unscrupulous line of action, and help the desired victory of Yudhisthira. 'You see king, I can this very day bundle all of them off to the Pandavas by sheer main force, it will stain me with no sin', Krishna rejoined, 'but I shall give myself up to no such common rage in your presence. I shall rather say the evil-doers just do the wishes of Duryadhana.'

When Krishna decided like that he had nothing to do just then. He only gave others in the assembly, especially Dhritarastra, to understand the gravity of the situation, he would not resist their vile attempts; an ambassador of peace, then only a guest at their place, was to be interned against all principles of hospitality and all codes of international diplomacy! In addition, he was not an ordinary emissary of truce, the Prime Fulfiller of the whole creation in flesh and blood, with all the superabundance of power over everything, yet with infinite mercy and love for all, even for the enemy. If the old king and his courtiers did not at once feel it in the manner quite expected, they were brought to that inspired state of mental prepossession by a kind of divine realignment of facts.

In an extremely enlightened state of mind Dhritarastra asked Vidura to bring Duryadhana there once more, he would make a final attempt to change his mind. When his arrogant son was accordingly led into their presence, the old king broached the infinite might of Lord Krishna and had a sharp dig at Duryadhana's abominably impossible design of taking him prisoner. It appeared to him as the unrealistic aspiration of a mere kid to reach down the unattainable moon. He was, in his exalted mood, practically descanting the infinite glory of the Lord, he was in the concentrated mental frame of meditation. All his analogies sprang from his very earnest attempt at realization of the All-powerful unique and incomparable essence of the Lord. Duryadhana was trying only an impossible feat. None was able to conquer Krishna, not even the combined army of gods, demons, Gandharvas and men : the dream would be as illusory as trying to take air with the palm of the hand, reaching out hand for the moon and as endeavouring to hold up the earth upon one's head. Dhritarastra contemplated the all-transcending power of Lord Krishna. Man's strength appeared too insignificant for comparison.

This mood of adoration and complete humility in Dhritarastra was hundredfold intensified by a similar and even more forceful broaching of that side of the Lord's glory by a more thoroughly realized person like Vidura. Vidura went on recounting some of the outstanding exploits of Lord Krishna and continued doing it in the most concentrated worshipful mood. Duryadhana must know from him how at the archway of the city of Souva, Dvibid the king of monkeys, in spite of all efforts and even after covering him in the hailstorms of stones could not take him. Even sixty thousand great heroes failed in their efforts to capture Krishna in the city of Nirmochan, rather they were themselves enshared at long last. In the city of Pragjyotish the great Narakasur in a joint campaign with the demons could not capture that Lord. 'Duryadhana, you are trying to achieve that inconceivable thing, to take that All-powerful, the ultimate stay of all life', Vidura murmured.

He did not end here, but turned to an enquiry into the prime cause of the whole Creation that Lord Krishna is. In his human existence, Lord Krishna started fighting the evil forces from his very pristine stage of childhood and conquered them all on earth. In his resplendent glory he excelled all the gods and their ruler. The divine mystery of the Lord's origin and his exploits are also touched by that meritorious devotee : 'He is the creator of everything that is, but not created by anything, the cause of all powers. He can do whatever he wishes, and for that he requires no effort' :

Ayang kartā na kriyate kāranang chāpi pauruse,
Yad yadichchhedayang shouristatat kuryādayatnatah.

(Ibid. Chap. 130, 51.)

He too in his prostrate state during the Deluge destroyed Madhukaitav. Vidura told Duryadhana, 'You have not known that Krishna the mightiest of the mighty and the most tireless Maker of all.' He saw his end was near as the insects' could be in the flaming fire.

While thus Vidura's mind and others' were held in sole concentration upon the mystery of Krishna's divine origin and presence, Krishna himself quipped in intensification of the same effect, 'Well, Duryadhana ! You have considered me alone and been encouraged to take me into your custody. But I am well-escorted yet by all these Pandavas, Brishnis, Andhakas, and even by the Rudras, Adityas and the great Rishis.' So saying he broke into a loud laughter, which made a physical as well as moral and spiritual effect.

There came a thousand changes creeping upon his body as if electric current of inconceivable depth and force held it in innumerable incandiscence. Blazing gods of small finger size continued to come out of it. From his forehead came Brahma, from his heart Rudra, from his arms all the rulers of the earth, and from his face came fire, Aditya, Sadhya, Basu, deities of the four winds, the twin Aswinis, Indra and all the thirteen protectors of the Universe. From his right arm appeared Dhananjaya, from the left Balarama armed with his plough weapon, and from the back Yudhisthira and his Pandava brothers and Prodyumma etc., Brishnis and Andhakas. All the lethal weapons of conch, wheel, club, and plough-shape appeared in front of Krishna in their terrible striking readiness; appeared also unidentified and unnamed many others from all sides. Tongues of fire with a crest of smoke blazed up from his nose, eyes and ears. And from pores of his body light glared like rays of the rising sun.

This rare revelation of Krishna's All-comprehensive omnipresence called Viswarupa was not visible to all, only to a selected few it was communicated by a sort of clairvoyance. It was conveyed through a psycho-spiritual channel to who may have been in the right reaction to it. The mythically relevant idea is, all the other kings and potentates except a chosen few could no longer see that revealed quintessence of the Lord's true presence :

Namilayanta netrāni rājāna strastachetasah.

(Ibid. 14.)

The Kshatriya kings who could have been there, closed their eyes in fear. This literal meaning of the sentence is quite suggestive of the impervious nature of their moral side. Only Drona, Bhisma, Vidura, Sanjaya and the great Rishis were given the eyes to see the revealed mystery of the Lord's being :

Rite Dronang cha Bhismang cha Bidurang cha mahāmatim
Sangjayang cha mahābhāgamrisīng shchaiba tapodhanān
Prādāt tesāng sa bhagabān dibyang chakshujanārdanah.

(Ibid. 14-15.)

While contemplating the divine essence of the Creator in his very mysterious aspects, the esoteric small group of the initiated stood in supreme communion with the Prime Cause of the Universe, recreating in their extremely extended powers of sense-perception all the inconceivable wonders even in the limited bodily presence of the Lord. It is all that concentrated force of passion emotion and sense reaction can effect in the exquisitely subjective devotional trim of the mind.

(5)

We know whatever their roles in the political powwow and war cabinet of the Kauravas Vishma, Drona, Sanjay and Vidura had a clear idea of a moral order centrally governed by a Prime Cause whose total representation in human form Lord Krishna was. Whatever their state policy and war strategy they looked upon Krishna as the absolute incarnation of Para Brahma, of course in their daily prepossession of other things that idea occasionally got beclouded, or awaited some suitable occasion to be sharpened. One such occasion undoubtedly Krishna's presence in the court room and his majestic grandiloquence and physical deportments must have offered. And these people were readily thrown into an unswerved contemplation of those divine traits of the Lord which they may have known in the Sastras to be associated with the Primal Being. These were really subjective recreations only objectively transposed, and so highly strung and so instantly transubstanstiated that they appeared in their living and telling forms.

It is, therefore, clear that everyone may not have that mental and emotional absorption, and that those who have that prospect might not experience it all at once and to the same degree of uniqueness. This is perhaps the reason why the blind king Dhritarastra could not have that thrilling experience right at that moment. But he wished he could have that rare gift—sincerely on that occasion when others were moved to so tremulous a passion beside him. He prayed to Lord Krishna, 'Lord, thou art lotus-eyed, best of the Jadavas, and the source of all good to the world, do me the only favour to grant me eyes to see thee alone and only for once, and nothing and none else in the whole universe, and granting that mayest thou revoke that gift of sight once for all.'

This must have been from no spirit of emulation but from the inmost yearning to see at least once that super-excellent revelation of the Lord's true being, in which he stood as the ultimate cause of the whole universe. Because of the humble petition the whole stray energy of the King's mind and feeling and even all his sensory nerves were at once roused to a unique concentration of intensified effect, giving it the keenest possible force of perception to conjure up for himself all the unqualified original qualities of the Lord in their living and voluble form. He was thus given an inward vision although he was externally blunted in that organ.

The old king, therefore, obtained eyes by the divine sanction of Lord Krishna, the eyes quite invisible by others and granted for the special purpose of realizing the Universal ubiquity of the Lord, called Viswarupa :

Adrishyamāne netre dve bhabetang Kurunandana

(Ibid. 19)

In the metaphoric and mythical sense of the word the old king by his own unqualified earnestness could revive that apparently lost power of spiritual realization, which is the only basis of further attainment towards knowledge of the Almighty Creator's presence everywhere and in all things. It is only a flush of the invisible eye, in Indian tradition called the third eye, the eye of truth, with a special power although for an absolutely short period of time, just the thousandth part of a second, by way of that unreserved pin-pointed concentration of all mind and soul upon the thought of the ultimate mystery of the Universe. The blind king, blind in every sense perhaps, could also enjoy that divine grace by the complete surrender to that only thought of realizing the Lord's true essence, his all-powerful all-comprehensive existence.

That a blind man could see entails the truth of a non-physical or supra-physical communication through an enormously extended aura of inner senses corresponding to those outer bodily ones, infinitely sharpened by an unswerved avidity of the mind which, according to the Indian concept, serves as the unfailing mediator between the two sets. Not all among the audience of the Kaurava court could see that divine revelation of the Lord, they had not that inner urge accomplishing that supreme concentration of the mind : not all those who could see were given that instantaneous vision or the perceptive awakening of the inner power of realization, which is also a gift, the sense organ of knowledge, at least the blind king was not given that power all at once, he was given that at a later stage, only when all his inner senses could be brought to a focus of intensified single mindedness for the singular experience.

Although at a later stage Dhritarastra saw the revealed glory of the Lord, self-created under the unique external impulse lent to his senses by the Lord's own divine gesture and in part by the other devotes' unreserved submission to his power and will. As it was mostly a self-created spiritual string of communion it was extremely of short duration, only a matter of a moment. Thus it is said that the Lord after that assumed his normal state and stature of his body :

Tatah sa purusabyāghrah sangjahāra bapuh svakam.

(Ibid. 23)

And he began to act as an ordinary man. He performed all the formalities of an honoured guest, exchanged civilities with courtiers and sought permission of the assembled Rishis to withdraw. He got near his chariot escorted by his men and the court elite; Dhritarastra just then said something, and the tone and tenor of his speech was by then quite changed, he was at that moment out of that state of devotional self-surrender; he simply assured Krishna as a well-meaning political leader of his sense of duty and responsibility :

'Lord thou art well-aware of the extent of my hold upon my

sons, and knowest also how sincerely I have tried to bring peace having no invidious intentions against the Pandavas.'

Lord Krishna too was out of that self-absorbed mood and met the changed attitude of the blind king as he was wont to do in a composed state of his mind. He told the king and all who were present, 'You have all seen what happened in the Kaurava court today, and how arrogant Duryadhana came to be and how Dhritarastra reported his lack of control over his sons. I do now accost you all to Yudhisthira's palace where I am presently taking leave to reach'.

It is an altogether different side of the Lord's revelation, just in his human form performing a common human duty. He was sent as an emissary to the Kaurava court. His mission failed, so he did the next alternative, he warned them about what was coming next. His Universal-I-state has also a human side with all the description and duties of a human being, only a part of an all-comprehensive whole.

KRISHNA'S RESPONSE TO A LAST PRAYER

This article deals with one of the very significant roles in which Lord Krishna had to appear in the Mahabharata. It has already formed part of common knowledge in almost every home of India, although the implication might not reach its expected unity. In this present analysis the realistic basis of the story is explored towards further strenthening of its spiritual import.

(1)

It is the end of the Kurukshetra war when Yudhisthira was celebrating his victory by means of gifts and attentions to those who deserved them. Then with an awakened sense of gratitude he came to meet Lord Krishna, but he found him in a mood and position never seen before. He prostrated himself before the Lord in humble submission, but the glorious figure in front of him paid no heed to it nor to his many words of solemn hymn sung in a spirit of absolute self-abnegation. In his shining garment Krishna appeared like an extra-brilliant gem wrought upon a gleaming piece of gold, and like a patch of blue cloud with its celestial sheen across a clear sky.

Yudhisthira saw Lord Krishna was completely absorbed in meditation, and all his external senses were withdrawn from outward responses into an extremely concentrated inward contemplation. He could hardly know what was the reason of it. There must have been something exceptionally disturbing somewhere in the three worlds claiming this singular attention, he thought. With absolute submission Yudhisthira expressed his desire to know the reason.

Krishna, as we all know, has the complete mastery over everything justifying his name Purna Brahma, the revealed state in entirety. So his withdrawal and engagement are all easily adjustable stages, sleeping and waking states are all one in that supreme actuality of revelation. So when he seemed to have been completely immersed in his soul he readily reacted to Yudhisthira's inquiry and received him with a gentle smile expansively to elaborate his reasons. Krishna told him how Bhisma in his last stage was sending his humble prayer to him. At the end of the Kurukshetra that great hero upon his bed of arrows set his entire soul upon him for mercy and salvation. So his mind went out of him to join him, only the outer cloak of his body remained where king Yudhisthira saw it.

This is another very salient feature of his creator's nature both in his revealed human state and unrevealed evanescence. He cannot withhold his love when one sincerely seeks it. He is always ready with a response even to the greatest sinner's call. Bhisma fought against the Pandavas even though he knew Krishna did not want it. It was Krishna in the battlefield who urged Arjuna to kill him, because he deserved it by fighting against Dharma, against the side led by the Lord himself for the values of life to be re-established. Now on his death bed when he prayed to the Lord for his soul's peace at the last hour Krishna could not but respond to it. He related to king Yudhisthira who won the war rightly how he felt for the dying. He revived in his mind the glorious past of the hero, and gave Yudhisthira to take note and make the best of it.

Bhisma is not only incomparably well-versed in the science of warfare but he is also a master of knowledge of every field; Krishna asked Yudhisthira to meet him on his death-bed and get the benefit of that knowledge before he died. This is also in the very nature of the Lord to speak highly of others' merits wherever he can and to pose extraordinarily ordinary in his normal course of life; he poses as if all knowledge has taken root in Bhisma, they should rather meet him for knowledge than for him personally. People are deceived not rarely by this pose in his common human roles; Yudhisthira is. He decided to meet Bhisma, it is quite proper he should, but it is quite a mistake that he should meet him for knowledge instead of Lord Krishna. It is curious to note that Yudhisthira, in spite of his knowledge of Krishna as the Supreme Being, not only made up his mind to take lessons of Dharma from Bhisma himself but also prayed that Krishna too should lead them there for the purpose.

Yadi tvanugrahabatī buddhiste mayi Mādhaba
Tvāmagratah puraskritya Bhismang yāsyāmahe bayam
(Santi Parba, Chap. 46, 28)

Krishna agreed to the proposal and immediately asked the chariot to be there for the trip.

(2)

Bhisma laid upon his bed of arrows is now surrounded by a large number of saints and sages from different parts of the land, crowding there to pay their last homage to the departing hero. But the dying general set his whole mind upon Lord Krishna, although he was not there yet, he was still preparing for the visit to the hero with the royal entourage. In the meantime Bhisma took no notice of anything else around him but was in a mood of single-minded adoration for all that he could call up of the infinite qualities and mercies of Lord Krishna. Many of his revealed traits flashed upon his mind in a state of absolute self-surrender. The Mahabharata deals with it in a very long passage, too long for a quotation. The essence of the passage, however, claims attention. Bhisma in his dying state cannot afford to think of anything but his own salvation. He knows there is no salvation without complete surrender to the Lord, he has left behind many mistakes by way of deviations from his path, from his wish, now is the time to do away with all that and to submit to him and him alone with all his mind and feeling, the only thing he could direct to this end when he has already reached the end of his life's activities.

It is natural that Bhisma should fix his whole mind upon Lord Krishna, the mystery of his incarnation and the secret of his Supreme Being as the prime source of creation. Although he was tempted in his life to act against the wishes of the Lord—he was then led by his own sense of the right—he knew that Krishna was the origin of all life and its ultimate end. In spite of this knowledge man can stray away from the known truth, Bhisma is perhaps one of its best examples. Even though Bhisma passed through some sort of obsession of this kind the known truth took hold of his entire consciousness at the last critical hour of his life, this is perhaps the best fruit of knowledge, the knowledge of the Lord's incarnation, of the path of virtue, of the source of grace and mercy. He is more secure than one who has no knowledge at all, at least he is better placed in this that he can seek the help where it can be found. Bhisma exactly did it, he knew where that ultimate help was in reserve for mankind, he turned to it in the hour of absolute need.

In this crisis of death-spasm he begged Lord to grant him his grace after this life's fitful fever :

Shuching shuchīpadang hangsang tatpadang paramestinam
Yuktva sarbātmanā ātmānang tang prapadye prajāpatim
(Ibid. Chap. 47, 17-18)

Bhisma's soul's prayer reached Krishna, however far he might be; soul's telepathy requires no other medium than utmost concentration upon its object. When Bhisma's mind was filled with thoughts of Krishna and had absolutely no wavering sentiments to disturb its calm, it was blessed with an unlimited power of vision. It came almost as a natural side effect, as every unreserved submission to the Prime Cause of creation brings with it. It was, therefore, quite natural that Lord Krishna would grant that gift to Bhisma at this last hour :

Abhigamya tu yogena bhakting Bhismasya Mādhabah
Trailokyadarshanang jnānang dibyang dattva yayou Harih
(Ibid. 102)

He gave him the power of the mind to see that link between the three states, past, present, and future, which means total knowledge of the three worlds.

(3)

Krishna was not still then physically present beside the dying hero who was already encircled by a great crowd of saints, sages and admirers. We know what led to Krishna's deciding personally to meet him in that state of extreme mental and physical crisis. Now he actually made the journey there accompanied by Yudhisthira and the other Pandavas and his close aides. When he reached the place where Bhisma was lying he found the latter in a posture of profound bow with his folded palms. It was directed to his divine self conjured up in his mind. The Lord knew it and quite appreciated the spirit.

While tripping down to that part of Kurukshetra where Bhisma was lying upon his bed of arrows, Krishna recollected the sad story of Parashuram's action twenty one times to extirpate Kshatriyas on earth and narrated it to Yudhisthira to satisfy his curiosity about it. They had already left their car behind. because driving was impossible among the heaps of dead-bodies and broken chariots. Yudhisthira was rightly in a mournful mood, but Krishna was supremely beyond and above that, unperturbed and well-composed. They took their seats around the gasping hero as the sages had already done.

Krishna then behaved exactly like an ordinary man, he gave none to be struck with his divine excellence. He addressed the dying hero with all sympathy of his heart to enquire if his senses were not dazed and knowledge obscured by the extreme pain of his body. He knew even a single prick of an arrow could cause great pain, and knew how great was the bodily pain when pierced by a swarm of arrows fitted with deadly tips. So it is useless to ask that. Krishna let him plainly understand that Bhisma's death at will was due to his own merit or derived from the boon of his righteous father, and not the result of an exceptional grace granted by him. He also gave Bhisma to note that he knew the mystery of sorrows and sufferings of this world, and the secret of life and death, he could even teach the gods about it. He would not spend many words upon the subject. So saying Lord Krishna changed the subject and spoke as if he were in a mood of worship towards Bhisma as the latter was towards him we have seen a little earlier.

The Lord told him the purpose of their meeting him. Yudhisthira was mournful because of the large scale massacre of his next of kin, he required consolatory lesson, Krishna thought Bhisma was the best man on earth to offer that, knowing all the Sastras and the secrets of the ways of the world.

Here one thing is particularly to note, Krishna decided to

see Bhisma at the instance of Yudhisthira; it was not then known that he had that object in view, rather a completely different end was suggested by Yudhisthira himself :

Darshanang tasya lābhah syāt tvang hi brahmamayo nidhih
(Ibid. Chap. 46, 30)

A sight of the Lord, the embodied Brahma, at this hour would do Bhisma good, that was king Yudhisthira's reason. But this suggestion came when Krishna asked him to meet Bhisma for knowledge, he then specified the field of enquiry in which, of course, this practical purpose was not included, we know. He asked the eldest Pandava to inquire mainly about the four departments of knowledge, Dharma, Artha, Kama, Mokshma—Ethics, Economics, Eugenics & Salvation—and something about politics and the four stages of individual evolution called the four Asramas. Then how came it to be that Krishna thought out this rather personal end and introduced it for attention ! The reason was not far to seek. Krishna wanted to serve a double end with the issue at hand. He is Purna Brahma with the equally complete mastery over both the visible and the invisible worlds. He knows best how to adjust the material world and the human affairs for good. He must have realized in that situation the need of consolatory interpretation of the whole issue of Kurukshetra for both Yudhisthira and Bhisma, even more for the latter in his last stage. Krishna would have kept silence over the matter with regard to Yudhisthira, he had already attached less importance to this side of the question and asked Yudhisthira to have knowledge of some more essential values of life; but when he saw Bhisma required some consolation in this acute state of physical mortification he served it in a subtle and indirect method by calling his attention to his own knowledge of the mystery for a lesson to the already complaining king Yudhisthira. It is rightly a measure of introspection for Bhisma and edification for Yudhisthira. Krishna made the best use of the situation for the good of all concerned.

Bhisma rightly pointed out that he was in absolute need of that eternal bliss of communion, the assurance of that favour at this last hour would settle all the stirs of his mind. He begged that favour of Lord Krishna, the final dispenser of all our destiny. Krishna readily granted that prayer, and even explained to him the meaning of his personal presence beside him that time. His physical response is not unwarranted, but in regular conformity with a spiritual principle. He told Bhisma that he could see his human form not without reason. He deserved it by his faith in him even from his early days. He reveals his divine person to those of unmixed faith and devotion, and not to those without faith, and not even to those who, although with faith in him, have a perverse nature and uncontrolled passions, Krishna made it clear to him. Let us quote below the verses purporting the idea above :

Na hyabhaktāya rājendra bhaktāyānrijabe na cha
Darshayāmyahamātmānang na chāshāntāya Bhārata
(Ibid. Chap. 51, 21)

Krishna came to visit him, in other words, to make him comprehensible to him in his manifested embodiment, because he led all through his life a restrained truthful and charitable round of daily existence. By his own virtue Bhisma merited the sight of the Lord's glorious presence, which frees man from the inevitability of the cycle of repeated birth and death. Although in the Kurukshetra he fought against truth and justice he sincerely followed a principle of self-control in his private life. All through his life he cultivated knowledge of both the material and spiritual sides of life, he knew Krishna was the Incarnation of the Supreme Creator and had always the deepest respect for him. The wrong that he did was that he could not come out of his priggish conceit of ethics for the person of the Lord who is, he ought to have known, the supreme expression of ethical values. But the Lord knew he had no hypocrisy, he only followed what he thought to be ethically correct, although he misfired owing to an oversight of another side of the issue. So he does not belong to that category of hypocritical devotees of the Lord (*bhaktāyānrijabe*). He was disqualified for the easy comprehension of the truth of the Lord's incarnated existence earlier for a different reason. Now at this stage he rightly deserved that knowledge and sight, because all his obsessions of the so-called ill-conceived ethics were gone, he had attained in its stead a state of complete self-surrender to the Lord himself. He then wanted only the Lord, in that crisis of absolute unavailability of help from any corner the lone support of his soul was the creator himself. So Lord responded to his prayer. He granted him life fifty-six days more. He granted it to make Bhisma and others derive the best out of that rare example of unqualified self-surrender, which only can solve all our problems at all levels including the inescapable crisis like death in human life.

(4)

Krishna then came to the point of what immediate benefit others could derive from that elevated mood of Bhisma. The mood was itself the greatest boon to its subject, and the longer it lasts the better for him. Krishna now gave Bhishma to know how the mourning king Yudhisthira could learn from him the highest lesson of life and morals when the mood had established a synthesis of all his already acquired knowledge of things temporal and spiritual. It would be a vicarious lesson to all mankind. Thus the proposal came :

Amung cha lokang tvayi Bhisma yāte
Jnānāni nangksyantyakhilena bīra
Atostu Sarbe tvayi sangnikarsang
Samāgatā dharmabibechanāya.
Tajnātishokopahata shrutāya
Satyābhisangdhāya Yudhisthirāya,
Prabrūhi dharmārtha-samādhiyuktang
Satyang bachoasyāpanudāshu shokam.

(Ibid. 17-18)

But Bhisma was not then in a mood to preach, not mainly because he was in severe physical torments owing to the sting of the hundreds of arrows, but particularly because he had lost that temptation, in such utmost devotional concentration of mind as this people do. Bhisma did of course casually plead his inability on physical ground. Bodily pain must be there, but his reason is he was eager to hear from Lord Krishna. He did not think that it was anything but sheer nonsense to talk knowledge when the ultimate source of all knowledge had revealed himself and was then present before them all. It is proper that Krishna should impart knowledge to Yudhisthira and all those who assembled there. He was the source of the whole Universe, and embodiment of the eternal principle, how could a disciple dare to expound the secret of knowledge in the presence of the preceptor himself ? Thus the verses run :

Kathang tvayi sthite Krishne shāshvate lokakartari,
Prabrūānmadvidhah karshit Gurou shisya iba sthite

(Ibid. Chap. 52, 13)

Krishna overruled his proposition intending otherwise to have it from his lips. The Lord knew Bhisma at this hour of crisis was blessed with a kind of rare spiritual awakening, which gave him a vision of truth and placed him in a position to communicate it to the world. The world cannot afford to miss this chance. So he granted Bhisma all that was necessary for the infallible transmission of truth through his agency. He would be relieved of all distempers of his body and mind. There would be no burning sensation of his wounds, no swoon, no daze, and no affliction of thirst and hunger. His mind would be free from all obsessions of passion and earthly attachment, rid of the two lower states of Tamah and Rajah, and attain the equilibrium state of Sattva. In this state of unique concentration of mind upon the Lord with unreserved love and dedication he would have as clear a vision of truth as a fish in water. To quote only a fragment of a long passage :

Sangsarantang prajājālang sangyukto jnānachakshusā
Bhisma drakshasi tattvena jale mīna ibāmale.

(Ibid. 21)

It is a moment of spiritual illumination even for the sages led there by Vyasdeva. They all rose for the worship of the Lord with a hymn of the Vedas sung in chorus, there were showers of flowers and drizzle from heaven to indicate the auspicious character of the event. Thus it came to be when the sun sank below the horizon, and Krishna with his entourage withdrew for the night. The sages too rose to get back their respective places of residence. Bhisma was left there with proper arrangement made for that.

(5)

Next day it is Krishna who took the initiative to meet Bhisma, he sent word for Yudhisthira to get ready. But earlier, we know, it was Yudhisthira who proposed Krishna's presence there beside the distressed hero. What's then the reason of the Lord's own eagerness to meet him ? The text has given no clear hint. Perhaps it would have been inartistic to be too prying in an epic grandeur like one the Mahabharata provides here. But a critical estimate cannot possibly omit or ignore the innate implication of the Lord's act. The Lord knows all good lies in him and man derives the best of it from unqualified love for his incarnated human existence and his unflinching faith in it. He cannot preach it himself. It will not only be repulsive to mankind but also set a bad example of self-praise, which, once adopted in man's own life, will surely block both material and spiritual furtherance. So the convenient method would be to utilize the exceedingly exalted spiritual passion in man himself, which, when it is in its truest nature, would reveal the truth of both love and faith for the instruction of his fellowmen. The Lord has always played this trick of his divine mission in his revealed state wherever he has been. This is one such moment and one such trick of the highest importance for mankind.

Now Krishna is all eager, his presence beside Bhisma will add to his urge in greater intensification of the mood itself. Satyaki was sent to Yudhisthira to tell him that Krishna was waiting for him. All the five brothers led by the eldest among them reached where Krishna was, and the latter accompanied by them drove immediately to meet Bhisma that morning.

It was now time to start the discourse. But who would ask questions for Bhisma to answer ? It was proposed by Yudhisthira that Krishna should initiate it, being the foremost in knowledge and wisdom among the assembled sages and princes from different parts of the land. So Krishna started exchange of common civilities with the hero and inquiry about the condition of his body and mind. In reply Bhisma let him know that through his blessings he had shed all the afflictions of his body and attained a rare clarity of vision in which he could discern the relation between things past, present and future, and the essence of all the various departments of worldly acquisitions; he was quite able to honour his request; but he did not know the reason why in spite of his presence there he should talk ethics to Yudhisthira. Thus Bhisma asked :

Svayang kimarthang tu bhabāngshreyo na prāha Pāndabam,
King te bibakshitang chātra tadāshu bada Mādhaba.
(Ibid. Chap, 54, 24)

We have already noted why Krishna avoided the course of edification himself, it would have been unpsychological and self-defeating to his purpose. Now to this direct question the Lord gave a twisted answer, the nature of his mission is a closed secret and should not be divulged even to the initiated. The state of Bhisma's mind lately assumed a special character conducive to the beatitude of communion and the communication of the already flashed truth in it. Krishna assured Bhisma that Yudhisthira had better get the secret truths from his mouth instead of his own only to ensure his glory on earth even after his death and till the end of time; and that all the kings and princes hailing from the four corners of the land would sing his glory ever afterwards for the lessons they would receive. Krishna did not deny the fact that he was the ultimate source of all glory and all good. So glory to him would be no attainment, no moving factor, neither to him nor to anybody else. He, therefore, thought of Bhisma's achieving it :

Yashasah shreyasashchaiba mulāng māng biddhi Kauraba

* * * *

Tathaiba yashasā purne mayi ko bismayisyati.
Ādheyang tu mayā bhūyo yashastaba mahādyute,
Tato me bipulā buddhi stvayi Bhisma somarpitā.
(Ibid. 25-27.)

In fulfilment of that end Krishna granted him all-comprehensive illumination or wisdom.

Bhisma had no cause after it to contradict or evade the responsibility just placed upon him. He felt more deeply than before that Krishna was the soul (Atma) of all that is and the only everlasting stay. He invited Yudhisthira to ask all that he wished of Dharma (*māng dharmānuprichchhatu*). Now at this stage Krishna offered to intercede. He told Bhisma that king Yudhisthira was ashamed to meet him after the extermination of friends and relations in war and was afraid of a curse he might pronounce. What Krishna just told him was factually correct, but Krishna might have offered it as an encouragement for Bhisma to immediately start his discourse in which the merits of Kurukshetra, its inevitability, would naturally be recounted. Exactly Krishna's initiative led that way; Bhisma readily assured Yudhisthira that he had done no wrong, rather he acted upon the true military ethics which a Kshatriya must observe, it formed part of his natural virtue.

Thus assured Yudhisthira took his seat beside the prostrate hero and began inquiries about different departments of human interest, which, although diverse in character, had the common springhead of Dharma. Krishna incarnated himself for this single mission, to teach the world Dharma, the principles of life and evolution, which he saw at his birth quite muddled up in other arrant overgrowths. The chapter opens where the principles are discussed always with reference to the Lord, the quintessence of all their living synthesis in one.

THE EVOLUTION OF KINGSHIP

The subject is traced back to an episode of the Mahabharata, Bhisma's discourse upon it in reply to king Yudhisthira's inquiry, A part of the article is an analysis and interpretation of the Sanskrit text.

(1)

We know Yudhisthira was still disconsolate at the large-scale death of near relations including his own brother Karna. He had no mind to enjoy the fruits of victory at the Kurukshetra. His own brothers, Vyasdeva and even Lord Krishna could not console him and bring him back to his royal duties. Now it is the turn of Bhisma in his exceptional mood of spiritual exaltation and grace to try once more to remove his grief. He explained to him the secrets of state principles (Rajdharma), quoting even eminent authorities like Brihaspati and Sukracharya. King Yudhisthira showed his interest in the subject, although not fully consoled yet. He wanted to know further how the institution of kingship came to be.

Bhisma took up the subject with keen interest and gave a fuller history of its origin. Yudhisthira asked him how of all men the king came to be an exceptional character and where did he get the power to rule the vast multitude alone being yet formed and endowed alike with all the rest ?

Shorn of all artistic niceties and the stretch of mythic apparatus Bhisma's account gives us a clean picture of a political evolution which mankind underwent in the course of thousands of years of their bitter experience. State first came into existence in the first of the four Ages called Satyayuga, Bhisma said :

* * * * *srinu sarbamashesatah,*
yathā rājyang samutpannamādau kritayugeabhabat.

(Santi Parba, Chap. 59, 13)

He narrated also how people had passed their days before some organized polity took shape. It was a life governed by natural laws, each person following his own natural instinct, the most fundamental of which was preservation of life and its furtherance to the fullest extent. This Bhisma called Dharma perhaps, at least his words convey that idea :

Dharmenaiba prajāh sarbā rakshanti sma parasparam.
Pālyamānāstathānyonyang narā dharmena Bhārata

(Ibid. 14-15)

It is evident that this was not the ideal state for mankind, that was not the beginning of its four cycles of eons taken into account in the ancient myths. People were then guided simply by their instinctive impulses which revealed the elements of Dharma; each one thought of his own personal safety and his personal good : this for some time, of course, maintained their mutual interest of life and living, Bhisma clearly stated...But it was purely left to the instinct itself, the other indispensable constituent of Dharma, the preservation of life and good of others as well as oneself, required organised discipline. There was yet no organized institution, social or political, to contain the dispersive trend that might develop. That an absolute reliance upon individual initiative and goodwill for the peace in the corporate life of the people is not safe enough was proved by later developments. Bhisma gave a similar account :

Khedang paramupājagmustatastān moha ābishat.

(Ibid. 15)

In the course of time, since they were undirected by any external institution, deviated from their healthy natural course and deflected into an obsessive self-love at the cost of other's good. Dharma no longer remained a living and life-giving principle which initially it was; it became a dead and morbid contemplation of exclusive individual happiness and narrowed the area of good from a sense of mutual cooperation to an absolutely selfish desire. It is not Dharma, a kind of self-seeking replacing the healthy idea of live and let live, conflict replacing cooperation. Then Bhisma thoroughly explored how gradually passion displaced the true principles of religion and made total havoc of peace in life. Infatuation obscured knowledge, men failed to see his true interest and his essential good, all the wrong desires of wealth, comfort and pleasures of the flesh made them blind to what was right. In the beginning, as Bhisma recounted, there was no king, no ruler and there was no punishment; people did not really think of that. But now in this state of total confusion of both Dharma and wisdom an urgent need was felt for some external power to restrain all bizarre deviations from principles.

Who are they that became awfully disturbed at this confused state ? Naturally those who were more conscious and who could not yet forsake the path of virtue, or had no mind to do. Normally they would be alarmed at the possibility of infection of evil. This exalted section of the whole creation, glowing with their devotion to the path of God in all particulars of their life was called gods (Devas) and was considered to have lived a plane above mankind, full of light and knowledge. Bhisma speaks of this saner segment of the creation, of course in full mythical aggrandizement of their glories.

The gods then approached Brahma, the Grandfather of the Creation, the remote cause of all life, for a remedy. With full knowledge of the state of things Brahma thought out a satisfactory solution of this problem.

Tānubācha surān sarbān svayambhūrbhagabāngstatah,
Shreyo ahang chintayisyāmi byetu byo bhīh surarsabhāh.

(Ibid. 28)

He assured them of his concentrated attention to it. In consideration of a remedy Brahma thought it necessary to evolve enunciated principles of every department of life for all men to follow so that none had to injure others' interest to achieve his own. These are the first codified laws of life that the world saw, a conscious attempt to ensure an organized society. But the book that Brahma compiled to make room for all the laws proved to be too vast for mankind, it was a book of one lakh chapters dealing with innumerable subjects, an account of which is almost impossible. But the purpose it was intended to serve is finally stated in all explicitness :

Deshajātikulānāng cha Dharmāh samānubarnitāh.

(Ibid. 71)

Here is the Dharma (nature) of the nation, class-division, and clan which is taken up for specification : on the basis of this nature and inherent efficacy (called virtue) the particular lines of their evolution are predetermined, the ultimate end of this book was to bring all these details within the knowledge of the people. But the plan was worked out so thoroughly that human life proved too short a span for its comprehension. It included all the four Bargas practically comprising all that was in life and all that was needed for the greatest prospect to be achieved individually and collectively.

The book that was thus compiled by Brahma himself is, in spite of all mythical grandeur, a necessary evolution serving one of the basic requirements of human civilization in its process of adaptation. The book was rightly called 'Danda Nity', the rules of Government. The political government which was not complete in itself was to be supplemented by regulations in all other spheres of life for its success. The guiding mind topping the entire creation must have seen the need and also the scope of an organised polity for the good of all.

The rules of the book were formulated, in other words, discerned operative in human nature. So it was an attempt to explore the mystery of nature. Seeing the vastness of this subject the future generation, rather the best mind among them, took upon himself the self-imposed task of condensing it into some basic principles of practical importance for mankind to observe. The task fell upon the greatest mind among the gods, the most enlightened Mahadeva. The best among the gods Shiva took the book from its original author Brahma, and considering the short span of life of the men of the world brought it within a comparatively limited compass of ten thousand chapters. He changed its title too to Baishalaksha. The attempt of adapting it to human application did not end here. Shiva only initiated the effort. The successive compilers and adapters of the principles took particular care to make it useful to human needs at different stages of the civilization.

After Shiva Indra took it for further abridgement, at a still later date the work was taken up by Brihaspati, the preceptor of the gods, for a compressed edition, and then a still further attempt at condensation of material was made by another scholar, Sukracharya, for the precise understanding of his contemporaries. In this way the knowledge of the principles of government was handed down to the successive ages from the original plan of Brahma to consider man's political life in a wider perspective of human values.

(2)

The fundamentals of government were already made out surely not overnight but in the course of long years of investigation and adverse experience. At a later stage, when already the rules of administration were stipulated, the need of a ruler was inevitably felt, and the more responsible section among the gods approached Visnu their leader for a ruler over the human society.

Atha Debāh samāgamya Bisnumūchuh prajāpatim,
Eko yoarhati martyebhyah shraisthyang bai tang samādisha
(Ibid. 87)

Lord, please appoint one who deserves to be called the best of the world—they made their humble appeal. Lord Vishnu who is entrusted with the protection of the world according to the triple division of charges in Indian mythology took it upon himself to make the choice, the entire security and prosperity of the creation depended on who would rule it after the divine constitution already in shape.

Vishnu considered whom he could appoint ruler over the entire human creation, but he did not find one in the whole world who was already endowed with all the virtues a ruler would possess. He saw a new personality with all the gifts of rare qualities would be presently created for this formidable task. He calculated in his mind all the best qualities the man should be born with and created him out of his mind as well ;

Tatah sangchintya Bhagabān Debo Nārāyanah prabhuh,
Taijasang bai birajasang soasrijanmānasang sutam.

(Ibid. 88.)

Curiously the name of that special creation was 'Biraja'. The man who was considered best suited for the charge had no desire to take it, a personality free from passion. He was neither born of passion nor involved in his life in one, he was born of 'Prajna' the content state of perfect wisdom. Vishnu contemplated the true virtues of the ruler of the world, of which a strong dislike for power and position for its own sake would be the chief one. Biraja whose name was significant had this innate disinclination. In the history of mankind the first human ruler was thus installed with the divine endowments of a perfect control over all obsessive passions and a natural disinterest in power and position. Biraja naturally did not desire the rule of the earth, his mind turned towards renunciation :

Birajāstu mahābhāgah prabhutvang bhubi naichchhat,
Nyāsāyaibābhabad bhuddhih panītā tasya Pāndaba.

(Ibid. 89.)

He is the beginning of a line of kings. He gave a child to the world called Kirtiman. He too inherited a part of his father's qualities, in him descended almost the same indifference to material comfort. Thus several generations passed with an uninterrupted rule of law, the kings well aware of the principles of government. A son, Kardama by name, was born to Kirtiman, and Ananga born to Kardama; this Ananga as we are told was well-versed in state principles. But the uniform evolution took an adverse turn in his son Atibal, up to his father the trend in the line was towards renunciation, their sense of justice could never have been disturbed by passion. But this trend became less and less strong from one generation to another. Possibly in Ananga's case the knowledge of the principles of governance attained greater importance than personal purity of life. Earlier in that line the kings were emotionally more concentrated upon self-purification and took less interest in wielding power. It would not disturb the balance if they paid equal attention to both these aspects, private life and public good. The trend was towards control over the public to a gradual neglect of control over their own self. That stage was reached during the rule of Ananga. The next stage of development was shown in his son's time. No doubt Ananga neglected the side of private morals, the rule of principles in his own life, he forgot that the king was not beyond the rule of law, that he should rather be the ideal example of it all.

Atibal, son of Ananga, neglected principles in his own life but took care only to impose them upon his subjects, which deteriorated into a sort of power tricks. He lapsed into a life of passion himself and fell wide apart from the original ethics of kingship.

Pratipāde mahārājyamathendriyabashoabhabat.

(Ibid. 92)

Atibal then marked a turning point in the development of the institution of kingship. It marked a sharp deviation from the God-instituted ethics of that great responsibility. In the next generation and next to next there was a further deviation from moral values against all laws of nature. Even the links in the next stage of development seem to have been somewhat obscure. We do not know immediately who Sunithā that daughter was, she is described in the Māhābharata as the 'Manasi Kanya' of Mrityu. Now should it be explained as allegorically symbolic ? Of course this sort of obscurity must have been suggestive in any case, any way the meaning must be in agreement with the trend in the line. Whether we explain her as an adopted child or born of some mental aberration, born to any person simply called Mrityu or born to a trend towards death, the fact remains in any case that the link is not sure, which gratification of reckless passion often causes, and that her birth bore testimony to a decline in moral values. That is why she cannot be clearly related to Atibal the immediate known predecessor in the line.

However spurious her relationship can be this daughter born in this line herself gave birth to an accursed child Ben by name :

Mrityostu duhitā rājan sunītha nāma mānasi,
Prakhyātā trisu lokesu yāsou Benamajijanat.

(Ibid. 93)

This Ben really became a bane of a king, morally distorted in his own private life naturally inheriting all devious tendencies from his parents' relation, which was perhaps a breach of the natural law. In ancient India the real guardians of all ethical principles based on human nature were the Rishis, people in constant communion with the ultimate Author of all life, so normally gifted with an insight into truth. They saw that the king had ceased to be the defender of the already established principles of life, himself ill-principled too; so they devised means of his downfall or dethronement.

Mantrapūtaih kushaijaghnurisayo brahmabādinah

(Ibid. 94)

They adopted an ancient hieratical method of extirpation which sought to avoid bloodshed and direct confrontation, their method led to a peaceful end of his life. By means of a sort of revival of the lost principles and ethical values initiated by a symbolic observance of sacrifice (Jajna) they secured the removal of the air of looseness and levity whose perfect embodiment the king himself was. This must have been considered as the death of his earlier self.

It was, however, not possible to get rid of the already muddled case of king Ben. He gave rise to a whole race steeped in all irreligious motives and tendencies. This is symbolically represented in the Mahabharata in that act of the Rishis who got the immediate successor to Ben from his right thigh degraded in nature and culture and also deformed in size and appearance, and stamped them as Nisada for all their blasphemy, devising means to keep them within safe limits.

Nisīdetyebamūchustamrisayo brahmabādinah.
Tasmānnisādāh sambhūtah krūrah shailabanāsrayāh,
Ye chānye bindhyanilayā mlechchhāh shatasahasrashah.

(Ibid. 96-97)

They left the natural habitat of Aryan culture and civilization and had their abode in wild forests and hills in thousands around the Vindyas and were known as savage, the verses here suggest.

They were thrown out of the confines of civilization perhaps to prevent contamination of rank barbarism.

The Rishis' concern was not only to eliminate the recusant element but also to inspire a sense of ethical discipline wherever that was possible, they treated the wicked king Ben with care to ensure both. They knew people already born of the evil tendencies of king Ben could not be corrected, they significantly came out of Ben's thigh, made to emerge from there, rather a fruit of his wanton desire. But there was also one who came out of another significant part of Ben's body with a healthy conformable tendency. The Rishis stirred the right arm of Ben for a person of completely different temperament and disposition; he was well-versed in state principles, well-read in the Vedas and their commentaries and quite immaculate in private morals.

It is seen that Ben was not entirely lost, he had still something which could be made to serve the good of the people. But the evil tendency which he inherited from a laxity in ethical principles in his parents made him often ill-principled; those born out of these wayward impulses were intractable in their evil preoccupations. But something that was healthy in him was directed under the care and attention of the Rishis on a right track and out of a properly chosen mate for him a healthy child was born. Ben died but his child remained as the future ruler of the people. The episode thus has this mythical implication. This is perhaps the reason for their choice of the expression (*Mamanthu*) :

Dakshinang pāning mamanthuste Maharsayah

This boy thus born was amenable to laws, he willingly submitted to the guidance of the Rishis in all matters private or public. He told them :

Mumūkshmā me samutpannā buddhidharmārthadarshinī

(Ibid. 101)

My desire for salvation has been awakened, and insight into the principles of religion and wealth.

Now he asked them what he should do with this awakened sense. He will do exactly what they will guide him to do. It is a complete submission. But the Rishis were not the people to guide wrong, to fulfil their personal end; they were in perfect communion with God, which gave them a true understanding of human nature and the general good of all mankind They asked him to rule the world according to the laws, they have found a worthy person for a king in him. The author of the Mahabharata has gone into details as to how he will discharge his duties as a king. The gods and Rishis enjoined that he should obey the principles of Dharma without any fear, mete out to every subject according to the laws without any favour; he should also shake off lust, wrath, greed and love for honour and all like intruding passions to judge and mend the deviations from the eternal edicts of nature already enunciated as state principles (*shashvad dharmamabekshatā*); and he should rule acknowledging the principles of Government, which may be called the divine constitution, the constitution not made for any particular individual or community but for the good of all. Further he should not punish the twice-born Dwijas, and see that children are not born of incompatible pairs (*barnashankarāh*). The Dwijas are to be kept out of punishment not for racial considerations, but for their cultural heritage and life-long preoccupation with it. If in any case there be any breach among them, any flop, it must be treated with all sympathy, their correction is otherwise enjoined culturally. The Brahmanas (not a caste as it may be misconstrued) are to be respected by the king and all, also for the same reason of their cultural attainments in society and their constant inquiry and engagement in human good.

(4)

Kingship with its original virtue and attendant responsibility is thus restored and the king who is thus entrusted with the rule of the world is named Prithu whom Visnu called the eighth creator. This king is now provided with some essential aids which were not earlier considered necessary. Practical experience revealed to the self-appointed guardians of human good, the Rishis, that the ruler himself was apt to deviate from principle and relapse into misrule. Although the Rishis remained the unofficial ordainers or law-givers, someone among them particularly well-versed in state principles was considered necessary to act as the official mentor called priest, Sukracharya the latest compiler of Dandanity held that post; some of the special type of Rishis called Balakhilya and members of the literati took charge of different departments as ministers : and the eminent Rishi Garga was appointed State Astronomer to read for him the changes of season round the year :

Purodhāshchābhabat tasya shukro Brahmamayo nidhih
Mantrino Bālakhilyāshcha sārasvatyo ganastathā
Maharsirbhagaban Gargastasya sāngbatsaroabhabat.

(Ibid. 110-111)

The king who might have been guided by his own whims and passions was now to be guided by a council of ministers. This is perhaps the first ministry to take part in the administration, just an evolution out of many years of experience of the Rishis.

Prithu was then ceremonially crowned in presence of the Rishis, gods and the Brahmins by Vishnu himself for the well-being and protection of the people. The king appointed his Governors from amongst his adorers and allotted Anupdesh to one such called Suta and Magadha to such another Magadh by name to carry on administration in his name. We have got here the principle of nomination of Governors followed now-a-days for provincial administration.

This Prithu is the perfect king unlike his ultimate forefather Biraja born of Vishnu's brain with a natural bent towards renunciation. Prithu was born to his passionate father only restrained and readjusted for a special cause purely of a sublunar nature, so born with qualities well-adapted to the mundane set-up. He was born with the best qualities of the brain as the great dynast of his line was, he was born with the strength of his arm, from passion, but passion well-restrained, not with renunciation but with actuated good. All these qualify him to be a king who could do immense good to the people under the guidance of the Rishis.

This truth of the king's excellence is not directly communicated, it is communicated through metaphoric application of myths. The king is here born in a line of divine origin, but divinity in a ruler of the world is not well-punctuated with renunciation, all that needs to be carefully reserved for the exalted dignity of a ruler is not withdrawal from the world, but a proper application of knowledge of the worldly affairs. The king is, therefore, to be born human in the line of a divine origin, which exactly conforms to Prithu's case. He sought all the material help from any corner for the efficient administration of the world and he got it. He exploited every possible source and applied all available resources for the good of the people with the readiness to use even force wherever necessary to enforce acknowledged principles. This is really the nature of a Kshatriya and not of a Brahmin. So Prithu, although coming down from a Brahminic tradition ultimately inherited all the Kshatriya virtues leaving off all the disqualifying elements that were his father's.

Ranjitāshcha prajāh sarbāstena rājeti shabdyate,
Brāhmanānāng kshatatrānāt tatah kshatriya uchyate.

(Ibid. 125-26)

He was called Raja (king) because all his subjects were well-content under his rule, he was also called Kshatriya for his proffered protection of all Brahmans (who were engaged in cultural mission) from injuries (kshata). Thus Vishnu himself enthroned the king as the ruler of the people, just his representation on earth, his offered protection to the world is to be extended through the king's agency; and enjoined that none would override him and his supremacy. And last of all Vishnu entered the king's self as if to ensure his greatness and the world's unquestioned allegiance to him :

Tapasā Bhagabān Bishnurābibesha cha bhūmipam
Debabannadebānāng namate yang jagannripam.

(Ibid. 128)

It is not to be considered a mere physical identification of Vishnu with the king; although like innumerable instances of the enigmatic style of metaphor often in use in the Mahabharata, it has passed for a myth yet the author seems to have taken some care in this case not to wander far into mere fancy. The word 'Tapasa' is to be noted in this connection. Vishnu entered him through his penance or cultivation of higher virtues. This is the most practical method by which restoration of godly element to human being can be best ensured. So it seems quite consistent that Vishnu should declare how the king can command respect of his subjects and how the kingdom can attain prosperity through his means. The king cannot expect that it will develop as a matter of course from the Lord's pronounced blessings upon him alone. He has to cultivate his inner virtues or acquire them for that :

Shubhang hi karma rājendra shubhatvāyopakalpate,
Ātmanā kāranaishchaiba samasyeha mahīkshitah.
Koheturyad bashe tistelloko daibādrite gunāt.

(Ibid. 170-71.)

All his acts should be good, actuated by good and for the good of all. The king is at the root of an achieved unity and a resolution of all discords. How can people surrender to his rule when he himself is devoid of reliable good qualities ? When all these are duly emphasized in the text one should know that the king's power is not a mere wind-fall, it is to be achieved through a proper synthesis of God-given qualities in him and his own acquisition in life.

When all these were ensured through Prithu's own sense of responsibility as a king all the gifts of Vishnu in him blossomed to perfection and for the uninterrupted well-being of the entire kingdom. From the king's personal evolution were derived the good fruits of Dharma, Artha, and Shri—peace, prosperity and opulence. Mythically all these came one after another from a lotus emerging from the temple of Vishnu himself. Came thereof Shri spouse of Dharma and Artha from Shri. It is an evolutionary process with the prime source of the king's integrated personality behind it.

Bishnorlalātāt kamalang soubarnamabhabat tadā.
Shrīh sambhūtā yāto debi patnī Dharmasya dhīmatah
Shriyah sakāshādarthashcha jāto Dharmena Pāndaba.

(Ibid. 131-32)

The author of the Mahabharata has no intention to conceal the literal meaning in the much too embellished myths of gods and natural phenomena. The truth comes as it does in the next verse in clear terms :

Atha Dharmastathaibārthah shrīshcha rājye pratisthitā

(Ibid. 133.)

Then are established peace, prosperity and opulence in the kingdom.

All these happened to king Prithu and his people. One might think it to be an exceptional case of special favour in care of the Almighty God. The dying hero Bhisma leaves no room for such a misleading notion, he recounts to king Yudhisthira the normal and natural course, the eternal truth of the natural selection of the ruler of the world...The king is selected by nature, he is not one perpetually belonging to heaven. By virtue of his own achieved merit he attains heaven, but in a depleted state of his virtue he is born later on earth well-accomplished in the rules of government. Such people inspired by the spirit of Vishnu came down to rule the world, they take upon themselves the protective and nurturing responsibility of the Lord.

Pārthibo jāyate tāta dandanītibishāradah
Mahatvena cha sangjukto baisnabena naro bhubi.

(Ibid. 134)

It is said that the king is established upon the throne by the Almighty himself. The implied sense is that the king is not chosen by men, as is done in modern democracy, but is accepted by them all as such, because of his excelling endowed merits, because of a sort of natural selection for the high responsibility self-imposed and self-acknowledged in his whole life and activities.

Politics took a different turn on Indian soil from its western evolution particularly in the ancient civilization of Greece and Rome. It was never guided by the frail and flexible wish of the people but was evolved for the good of all of them under the infallible guidance of the Rishis. At one stage the evolution seems to give the idea of divine choice as it was conceived in some section of the Western political philosophers and as it was acknowledged in the Mediaeval period of English history too. But the Indian scene was of a different colour, divine it got to be for universal good, as God is conceptually the ultimate source not only of the origin of all life but at the same time the ultimate source of all their good. India had accepted that idea from the very beginning of the evolution of the state. They thought of someone who could, by virtue of his higher qualities and greater control of passions and propensities, safeguard safety and prosperity of all without any exception under the constitution of natural laws taken into consideration by the seers of the land for the unique and individual evolution of everyone in close harmony with their collective good.

In ancient India all knowledge was sought to be derived from a single source, the one and indivisible source of the mystery of Creation, the ultimate cause of this visible universe. The ancient Rishis sought to have knowledge of that fundamental truth of life and existence of all, this inquiry took a supra-scientific method of inner cultivation called Tapasya, and the result of such Tapasya was Veda (knowledge) which was further classified up to their time of realization into four major provinces still further subdivided into numerous branches at a later date, and declared to be 'Apourusheya' (of no man's creation) having no end to its extent or scope.

Political or otherwise ancient India acknowledged but one constitution, the enunciated principles out of that overall mystery of life and creation as far as human inquiry could go in endless scope of ever expanding Nature. The Rishis took that responsibility upon themselves and asked the king to be guided by the already realized knowledge envisaged in that constitution which was called divine and proverbially declared to be derived from the Creator himself for the good of all. It concerned and covered the highest good of all and it was accepted as the best form of democracy. It was called democracy in ancient India not because it was ruled by the demos (which understood to have conveyed the aspiration of the people) but because in that rule their true interest was ensured.

A HOAX THAT WAS PROMPTED

Krishna is known as the master of tricks, but he played them only to achieve as much good as the situation may allow, which otherwise could not be achieved. One of the most blameable of them which he encouraged was the trick of causing Dronacharya's death. The present article seeks only to see how it came about and what impression it makes.

(1)

One of the fiercest assaults in the Kurukshetra was the attack that Drona made upon the Pandavas. The exceptional predicaments in which the Pandavas were then arose from their having to fight directly against their Astra-guru (war guide). Earlier when Arjuna, the best of the disciples in arms, had to lead the army against his preceptor in warcraft it was rather a worthy scene of the best skill in warfare than of havoc of killings. No kill-joy it was, rather it drew praise of all men and gods alike. Even Dronacharya felt proud of his disciple's skill, even though he would have fallen a victim to it. Although apparently dangerous, the nature of their armed engagement ultimately proved nothing but a sport, only a demonstration of the highest military skill. But Kurukshetra is a war that sought to re-establish the lost values of life, so it earned the alternative name of Dharmakshetra—a (battle) field of Dharma.

But all along in the field things did not go so well and so easy. Dronacharya is a master of all arms, well-versed in their use, he made havoc of all lives, men and animals employed in war. When it is not an encounter between Drona and Arjuna things altogether changed; men and materials were destroyed in their thousands by that old hero's war-tricks. Now the problem before them was to save life. Drona was indiscriminate in the massacre of lives before him, at this rate of casualties the Pandava army would soon be extinct. The situation worsened considerably because of the respect-psychosis that had already seized the minds of the Pandava brothers, particularly Arjuna. Drona had some affection for the sons of Pandu, all of them his disciples in the use of arms, that affection acted as a restraining force in the fight against the Pandava army. Only when it is a single fight as between Arjuna and himself such an affectionate sentiment played its intensest part. If the war continued like that as he began no doubt the whole Pandava army would have been extirpated, leaving, of course, the five brothers only to be done in by other heroes on the Kaurava side. The Pandavas did not see it, there is much reason to conclude that they did not, but the all-seeing Lord knew the consequence. So it is he who raised the issue and suggested the way of escape :

Matimān shreyase yuktah Keshaboarjunamabrabīt,
Naisa yuddhe na sangrāme jetung shakyah kathanchana,
Sadhanurdhanvinang shresto debairapi sabāsabaih.
Nyastashastrastu sangrāme shakyo hantung bhabennribhih

(Drona Parba, Chap. 190, 9-11)

He suggested to Arjuna, 'The leading among those armed with missiles and charging instruments he (Drona) is not likely to be overpowered in skirmishes or war even by gods with Indra as their leader; but he is apt to be slain by men only when he lays down arms in war.'

Thus Krishna offered the clue as to how they can win the war and get rid of Drona. He did not end by a mere hint, he of course explained the moral basis of such an incitement :

Āsthīyatāng jaye yoge Dharmamutsrijya Pāndabāh.

(Ibid. 11)

The Pandavas must shun all their moral scruples and adopt some tricks. The term Dharma is here misleading, not used in its original sense of the principles of life, but as some moral considerations to which the Pandavas have lately fallen victims without knowing the full implication of their logic. Nothing escapes the notice of the omniscient Lord. So the Lord foresaw elsewise their total extinction.

Yathā bah sarbān na hanyād rukmabāhanah

(Ibid. 12)

In order to avoid that terrible end the Pandavas must employ some tricks, and the tricks too are suggested by Lord Krishna :

Ashvatthāmni hate naisa yudhyediti matirmama
Tang hatang sangyuge karhchidasmai shangsatu mānabah.

(Ibid. 12-13)

Krishna told them if Drona could be persuaded to believe that Asvathama was dead he would no longer fight in the battlefield, so someone must declare that he was killed in battle.

It is an innocent trick to declare one to be dead who is not, a sort of white lie, designed only to escape a real pother. The preceptor cannot otherwise be restrained or overpowered in his fury of killing. Krishna has not immediately asked any of the Pandavas to kill their preceptor. But Arjuna did not agree with him, directly he refused to adopt such a method. No doubt it was repugnant to his sense of the right, but it is not difficult to see that he lost all sense of life in a disproportionate exaltation of his idea of military ethics. He took no account of the consequence.

The other heroes on their side quite appreciated the suggestion that Krishna made, and Yudhisthira was only persuaded with difficulty to accept it. Bhima took the initiative to implement the tricks. He first clubbed to death an elephant of their own army Asvathama by name, and then approached Drona shamefacedly to declare that Asvathama was dead. He thus wanted to mislead Drona to understand that his son was dead. Although Drona was at first shocked to know it he soon recovered his strength and energy, thinking that an unconquerable hero like his son would not so easily fall, and doubly infuriated by a sense of immediate danger began to use his arms with redoubtable spirit against his death-like enemy Dhristadyumna, who was closing in with his twenty thousand well-trained soldiers. The result was the end of all the twenty thousand soldiers from Panchal under Dhristadyumna's command. Drona was so mad with the furies of war that he spared none and nothing, not even the innocent animals employed in the fight :

Punah panchashatān matsyān satsahasrāngshcha Srinjayān,
Hastināmayutang hatvā jaghānāshvāyutang punah.

(Ibid. 31)

Along with the allies like Matsyas and Srinjayas killed in hundreds and thousands, millions of elephants and horses were also slain. The large-scale massacre of both men and animals, not all properly trained in the art of war, caused by a man who was universally acknowledged as the master of the military science, led all to think seriously of the consequence. Even the Rishis could not stand this massacre of the innocents. A host of them thus appeared—Viswamitra, Bharadwaj, Jamadagni, Goutam, Bashista, Atri, Vrigu, Angira, Garga, Balkhilya—all those great and small repositories of sacrificial fire, were shocked at Drona's attempted total extinction of the Kshatriya race. They addressed him with wards of warning and short interpretation. To avoid a long passage I quote below only snatches of their comments :

Adharmatah kritang yuddhang samayo nidhanasya te.
Bedabedangabidusah satyadharmaratasya te,
Brāhmanasya bishesena tabaitannopapadyate.
Brahmāstren tvayā dagdhā anastrajnā narā bhubi

(Ibid. 35, 37, 39)

The Rishis called his attention to a serious point. He was fighting with least consideration of morals, so it was a sure portent of his fall. He was well-read in the Vedas and their supplements, always on the path of virtue, and particularly a Brahmin; it behoved him ill to act like this. He was inflicting blows of all invincible arms upon those who were quite ignorant of their use. The Rishis expressed their deep consternation at these reckless killings; they repeatedly drew his attention to the fact that he was a Bipra by caste, Brahmin in attainments and a twice-born called Dwija : their stress on the caste is not without meaning. Drona was then behaving in an abnormal way, war is a science of study, which could very well be taught by a Brahmin when teaching belongs to his normal province, but a Brahmin cannot fight like a Kshatriya. Division of labour in those days was not an imposition but an evolution of the deep-laid instinct of different classes, which was universally respected and strictly observed in ancient India.

Drona forgot all these acknowledged edicts of society in a rage. Now that the Rishis advised him restraint he relented. He had already doubted the truth of Bhima's proclaimed information of his son's death, his son, he thought, was not a callow stripling so easily to be eliminated. At the warning of the Rishis he gave a second thought to this moot point. He would then go for a verification of the floating rumour of such a pitiful incident. He thought about a reliable source and was convinced from his knowledge of Yudhisthira's life from its very early stage that he would not at least prevaricate for any advantage. So he decided that he would ask Yudhisthira about it. We know from what happens in the Mahabharata that Yudhisthira would surely have done it had he not taught otherwise by no other person than Lord Krishna himself.

(2)

Yudhisthira had hardly any idea of the strategy of war, at least he gave no evidence of any in the whole course of the events, even the Pandavas scarcely gave any remarkable proof. The whole of the war strategy was planned by Lord Krishna, they fell where they ignored his idea. It is a crucial moment for the Pandava army in the face of the superior science of war ruthlessly brought to an act of killing by a master of that science, the whole army is totally routed, their strength is hopelessly reduced by the huge loss in men and material, only a surviving skeleton of it is fighting like a shaking reed on the front. Lord Krishna foresaw it all, and to avoid such a situation he advised them to ward it off by a trick, also a part of their strategy. But they took no notice of it, only Bhima who was not very punctilious about his sense of morals acted unsuccessfully upon it. Drona found no reason to give credence to his acts and words.

In this crisis of their position Krishna thought it indispensably necessary to sound Yudhisthira once more, when it was known that Drona had at last relented under the warning of the Rishis and wished to ask Yudhisthira for the truth of the already circulated rumour. Krishna took the chance and approached Yudhisthira to explain to him the graveness of the situation, which almost escaped his notice in a sort of pious stupefaction of prudish inflexibility. Krishna told him that at this rate of loss the whole army including the Pandava brothers would be entirely efaced from the earth within half a day, and the only means of escape still open to them was a trick of a lie which would be made convincing to Drona by his very word of mouth. He knew Yudhisthira would be very particular to avoid lie, although without knowing the whole secret of it. So he explained also how far the issue in hand involved falsehood and sin.

Yadyardhadibasang Drono yudhyate manyumāsthitah,
Sat͎ang brabīmi te senā bināshang samupaisyati.
Sa bhabāngstrātu no Dronāt satvājjyāyoanritang bachah
Anritang jībitasyārthe badanna sprishyateanritaih.

(Ibid. 46-47)

Krishna told him that it was he who could save all of them from total annihilation at the hands of Drona, in this case falsehood was better than truth, and to tell a lie for life would not implicate one in a sin of falsehood. We know even the Rishis asked Drona to lay down arms and desist from killing (*Nasyāyudhang rane Drona*) Krishna's intentions were perhaps to neutralize Drona's destructive vehemence, any way to make him lay down arms. It became a life and death question, either do it or die the whole lot.

At this stage of Krishna's persuasion Bhima, who had already tried to play the trick, narrated how he had done it by killing an elephant of the name Asvathama in the battle. And then he asked his brother Yudhisthira to take the hint from Krishna's very helpful suggestion and proclaim to Drona their preceptor the news of Asvathama's death for an immediate effect upon the fighting hero, he would surely trust his words, he being famed in the three worlds as a teller of truth.

Yudhisthira now considered the suggestion well in his mind and brought himself at last to act upon it. But he could not still then get rid of his fear of untruth, so

Ashvatthamā hata iti shabdamuchchaishchakāra ha.
Abyaktamabrabīt rājan hatah kunjara ityuta.

(Ibid. 55.)

he pronounced 'Asvathama is dead' and correeted it in undertones, 'an elephant'.

Obviously Yudhisthira played the trick even more trickily than Krishna suggested. It was so because Krishna's sense of falsehood and his sense of it were quite different. Truth or falsehood whatever it was, it must not be considered apart from its role in a complex phenomenon of life, Krishna felt. Yudhisthira would not at all consider it in a wider perspective of values, which life demands. In his view truth and falsehood are isolated phenomena, such an attitude is fundamentally wrong and a dangerous unreality in the very scheme of Creation. Yudhisthira was then obsessed in that pious illusion as he was very often on similar other occasions in the whole of the Mahabharata. So when he declined to use a trick to save so many lives he unwittingly committed a sin, and when he persuaded himself to save them ultimately by a simple lie he added a further sin of hypocrisy under obsession. Krishna knew this was not truth, truth cannot be against life and its unforced natural prospect, all that is against the normal course of life and its evolution is surely false.

Yudhisthira had no knowledge of this secret, he did not even care to learn it from Lord Krishna, and followed the mirage of his morbid sense of truth. Even when he would unwillingly do a little justice to the claim of life, exactly under utmost persuasion, he unconsciously relapsed into his old infirmity. What he did now he did purely just as a weakling would have done with no heart but a sense of wrong. So he partly righted the wrong as he thought by a hypocritical pose which just escaped his notice. It was a more grievous sin than lying, and its grievousness was instantly recorded in a sharp reaction in nature.

Tasya purbang rathah prithvyāshchaturangulamuchchhritah
Babhūbaibang tenokte tasya bāhāh sprishanmahīm.

(Ibid. 56)

Before that Yudhisthira enjoyed some special status even in war, his chariot kept hovering four fingers' measure above ground; but now that he spoke this his special privilege was withdrawn and the carrier at once touched the ground.

The privilege was taken away not because he spoke a lie, but because he spoke in a manner that showed him sufficiently devious and distorted in his attitude and even in his sense of the truth. What he was then doing was not considered by him as a sacred duty, it was considered a crime which was sought to be counterbalanced by a piece of cunning; there is in it neither courage nor piety, he is here as a double-dealing imbecile who will ensure a secure place for him in heaven by any means, if possible, even by smuggling purity. Nature cannot possibly stand such a sham religiosity.

No doubt Lord Krishna did not want him to do it like this. Any way he did it at last The deed done had its two-fold impact : one upon Yudhisthira's personal integrity and the other upon Drona; Yudhisthira came down in the scale of virtue and Drona believing his son dead laid down arms upon his chariot and was in a grievous mourning mood. He gave up all desire for life, and in his resigned mood he remembered the Rishis' warning and his offence towards the Pandavas. Just when he was revolving all these in his mind he saw Dhristadyumna before him to his utter dismay and disturbance of mind. He could not at once and ever fight as he did earlier.

(3)

There is practically no role of Lord Krishna in the actual killing of Drona. Never did he instigate any one directly to kill Drona, he only asked them to make him inactive so that thousands of lives could be saved and the side of truth and justice conld win. But death inevitably came as it was decided by Fate, which, of course, did not work blindly as it is thought it did in Greek literature. Dhristadyumna was born out of the sacrificial fire for some special purpose, we know. The Pandavas being all pupils of Drona would not agree to kill him, even the sentimentally coarse among them Bhima too might not have his way to do it. Then who will meet him in war ? Naturally someone who may not have such moral obligation. When Drona is to be eliminated for the cause of virtue, he fights on the side of vice, nature will take its own course to have it done, which is practically the work of Fate in the Mahabharata. So Dhristadyumna's miraculous birth, although mythically explainable as being in the course of much sacrifice to gods, was predestined to serve this special purpose.

Dhristadyumna was in no predicament to face Drona, normally he would take this responsibility of his own accord when it was dangerously neglected by the Pandavas : and Drona too would take it quite easy when fighting against his own pupils and be alarmed to face one who had no moral scruples to fight him out. Thus it happened when Dhristadyumna appeared before him. He was not fighting like the Pandavas and Drona knew he would not spare him even though he might lie prostrate upon his chariot with a heavy heart. When he saw Dhristadyumna take a choice missile to charge it against him he thought his end was near :

Tamisung sanghatang tena Bhāradvājah pratāpbān,
Dristvāmanyata dehasya kālaparyyāyamāgatam.

(Ibid. Chap. 191, 7.)

So he exerted himself to resist him, but in vain. He found that all his choice weapons he had already exhausted in his reckless fight over four days and a part of the fifth. Again he was thrown into a gloom and a sulky mood, reminded once more of the word of warning by the Rishis. He lost half his desire to fight and faced the enemy not exactly without any effort of reprisal, but in diminished vigour. He made a choice of that weapon, the hallowed gift of Rishi Angira, and aimed it at Dhristadyumna. So the popular view of Drona's complete renunciation of arms and war-path in utter dejection of heart is not supported by the text. He did not refrain from doing what he could in that extremely awful handicap. The weapon that he discharged selecting from his reduced stock hit the enemy right to destroy his propeller ready for use, the propelling instrument, the spire of his chariot and the charioteer himself. Thus frustrated in his almost decisive attempt Dhristadyumna made an alternative choice of both arms and instrument for the next attempt. This attempt was also baffled by the use of a rather crude missile called 'valla' which could only be used at a close range. Perhaps for shortage of stock Drona could make no better choice :

Bhallena shitadhārena chichchhedāsya punardhanuh.

(Ibid. 16.)

Whatever there was in that exhausted stock Drona made the best use of, and made up for the arms' lower capability by his extraordinary manoeuvre. He brought Dhritadyumna to a deplorably desolate state by destroying all his arms he held in his hand except only the club and the sabre, by knocking down all these with irresistible nine missiles.

In this pitiable state Dhristadyumna played another trick. He drove his war horses in among Drona's whole lot to make a bewildering mess of a target. But the trick could not be effective, because Drona distinguished his own horses by their colour and made a massacre of the enemy steeds. In a tight corner like this Dhristadyumna saw no other way but to fight him at a close range with his sabre protected in a leather buckler, taking to all the twenty-one kinds of physical movements to dodge the enemy aim. He was then fighting within his arms length and Drona had to discharge short-range propellers, which only a limited number of heroes like Kripa, Arjuna, Karna, Pradyumna, Satyaki and himself knew how to use, to hit him at half a cubit's distance. It could have been quite fatal to Dhristadyumna had Satyaki not come to his help in time to cut the missile midway with his weapon. Thus he saved him in presence of non-participating observers of both the sides to their despair or delight as the case may be. Among those who were delighted and heaved a sigh of relief at his safety were Krishna and Arjuna. Particularly Arjuna drew Krishna's attention to the uncommon skill of

Juyudhana (Satyaki) which awakened wonder in all, in himself and all his brothers and soldiers on their side.

At the intervention by Satyaki the fight no longer remained a single fight between Drona and Dhristadyumna. It provoked a mass-participation. Kripa, Karna and the Kauravas who stood aloof watching the course of the fight hastened to an attack against Satyaki. The Pandava brothers, Bhim, Sahadeva and Nakula saw the danger and formed a ring round Satyaki to repulse a multi-pronged assault upon him. It was then Yudhisthira who asked their men to close in and spring an attack upon Drona to the striking hero Dhristadyumna's help, for he thought Dhristadyumna would in his rage surely bring an end to the preceptor's life. At his command all his allies engaged in a terrible fight. Drona too did not back out, he saw some evil omens, a shiver ran down the left side of his body repeatedly, even his horses shed tears from their drooping eyes. He once again recollected the words of warning by the Rishis, but yet he could not withdraw from the field, quite despaired of all hope of life he fought rather desperately and caused heavy casualties on the enemy side. Dhristadyumna was reduced once more to a helpless and hopeless condition having nothing to fight with. In this forlorn state Bhima took him upon his chariot and provided him with the mightiest of propellers at his disposal and said something not merely by way of encouragement but of special significance :

Na tvadanya ihāchāryang yoddhumutsahate pumān,
Tvarasya prāg badhāyaiba tvayi bhārah samāhitah.

(Ibin. Chap. 192, 28)

None other but you can meet the preceptor in an encounter, so be quick, you are predestined to the onus of his end—so saying Bhima inspired him. For some special reasons noted above the Pandavas were unlikely to do the job. The truth that Bhima spoke although apparently as words of encouragement worked well. Dhristadyumna armed afresh with a supply of weapons from Bhima fought with a terrible force, but he was struck deep upon his breast and was dazed with acute physical pain. What Bhima did at this unexpected blow was suggestive of his very character.

Among the Pandava brothers Bhima was comparatively a little coarse in his manners and sentiments : although he would not personally kill the preceptor, he wanted him dead particularly at this point of great strategic failure and massacre of lives. Dhristadyumna's defeat was then considered by him a great set-back, his death would surely deprive them of the means of escape from Drona's wrath. So Dhristadyumna's stupor was taken very seriously, his ire burst into harsh reproach towards the preceptor, but in spite of its harshness it revealed a truth :

Yadi nāma na yudhyeran shikshitā brahmabandhabah
Sakarmābhirasangtustā na sma kshatrang kshayang brajet,
Ahingsā sarbabhūtesu dharmang jyāgrastarang biduh,
Tasya cha Brahmano mūlang bhabāngshcha Brahmabittamah
Shvapākabanmlehchhaganān hatvā chānyān prithakbidhān
Ajnānānmūrhabad brahman putradaradhanepsayā.
Ekasyārthe bahūn hatvā putrasyadharmabidyayā,
Svakarmasthān bikarmastho na byapatrapase katham.

(Ibid. 37-40)

If the people of Brahminic ties, yet discontent with their natural occupation, did not fight well-trained in the art, there could be no extirpation of the Kshatriyas : enmity to no creature is considered a living virtue, which constitutes the central point of culture of the Brahmins and in you most being the foremost of them all : why are you like a low-born Chandala (Pariāh) and like one quite obsessed and ignorant, and in realization of the only object, the interest of your wife and children, and of wealth, destroying many who are in place in their natural occupation, yourself displaced from your destined part, simply to secure your son's welfare, and yet not feeling ashamed ?—thus Bhima went on. He also reminded him that he was fighting an already lost battle, his son for whom he was fighting and whom he was eagerly awaiting had fallen in the rear, as the righteous Yudhisthira had long before told him. He had never doubted his words, why was he not convinced then ? Among the brothers Bhima is the least scrupulous about the delicate moral issues of life, he is too dashing for that. So he did not at all seek any moral support for the lie he had to tell.

His reproach worked. Drona finally decided to desist from war. He called upon other generals on his side and asked them to take charge of the army in action, for he would fight no more. He mentally prepared himself for the last journey and proclaimed 'no fear' to all living creatures.

Dhristadyumna took advantage of this renounced state of Drona's mind. He approached his chariot armed with deadly weapons and overpowered him. But he did it at a moment when Drona was meditating upon the Supreme Soul (Para Brahma) heedless of anything around him. He concentrated all his mind and feeling upon the thought of the Prime Being (Purana Purusa) and his embodied expression Basudeva and thus gave up the ghost in the deepest communion with that Cause of all causes. Dhristadyumna hardly knew it, he was mad with war fury and in the spirit of final retaliation severed that head of the lifeless body to the utter dismay of all around him.

None on the side of the Pandavas wished such cruel treatment of the preceptor, among them Arjuna first raised the cry of dismay and repeated word of utmost appeal to Dhristadyumna for not slaying the honoured teacher of the science of war and for bringing him alive there. Other generals of their side, too, resounded the same appeal. Arjuna in his last attempt ran towards Dhristadyumna to prevent him but in vain. Dhristadyumna did the most gruesome deed, shocking to both friends and enemies. He took the severed head of Drona, flourished it in the air, even himself besmeared with its running blood, and at last flung it away before the enemy troops who at once fled for fear of life in all directions.

Just before Drona's death he attained the most lucid moment of his life, he entered a state of complete renunciation; although the news of his son's unexpected death threw him into deep despair he must have overcome that depressed state for an enlightenment in anticipation of his inevitable end, particularly when he was reminded by Bhima of his nature-ordained avocation. He concentrated his whole mind and heart upon the thought of the Supreme Cause and shuffled his mortal coil even before one could touch him from the enemy side. The secret of this enlightened mood of complete resignation could not be known to an infuriated soldier like Dhristadyumna drunk with all the furies of war. Only a few people knew it, of them the narrator of the story was one. Krishna perhaps wanted such a peaceful end, rather he foresaw the prospect. He is the master of the world and the world beyond, in his adjustment of things to the highest possible good of all he takes into account both. So to secure the good of the righteous he wanted Drona's end in this world and a fresh start in the existence beyond, called heaven, for his good too. People only saw Krishna's tricks, but they did not see the truth behind it. All Drona's prospects had come to an end, his existence here would be tormenting to the good people of the world as it had been, for his further evolution a different set-up was necessary, he was then provided with that. His transport to a higher plane of existence was witnessed not by all, it could not be, but by only a few, particularly Lord Krishna :

Bayameba tadādrākshma pancha mānusayonayah
Ahang Dhanangjayah Partho Kripah Sharadvatastathā.
Bāsudebashcha Bārsneyo Dharmaputrshcha Pāndabah.

(Ibid. 56-58)

NARAYANASTRA : WHAT IT WORKS

This episode of the Mahabharata is closely related to the story of Dronacharya's death dealt with earlier. Both the article taken together would reveal the truth behind the apparent irregularity in the whole course of the events thereof.

(1)

Dronacharya died at the age of eighty-five. His son Asvathama inherited from his father a lot of deadly weapons with the science of their use. Drona had them from his war-preceptor, Parasurama. Now that he found his son quite worthy of such a rich possession, he relegated the whole lot to his care and use in times of exceptional need; among them the choicest item was Narayanastra. But Narayanastra had not only this exceptional capability but also its uncommon origin. Drona got all his training from his Guru, but this weapon of irresistible force he received from Narayan himself, the supreme guide of mankind.

The story of how Drona received it is quite significant. One day, why we do hardly know, Narayan in the guise of a Brahmin came to meet Drona who accosted him respectfully and honoured him with a present. Then the Brahmin well-satisfied with it wished to grant a boon. Drona prayed at this that he should grant him Narayanastra if he so pleased, and that Brahmin granted it.

Tang svayang pratigrihyātha bhagabān sa barang dadou,
Babre pita me paramamastrang Nārāyanang tatah
(Drona Parba, Chap. 195, 32.)

The text has nothing more than that. It is rather a strange coincidence that Drona should ask Narayanastra from Narayan himself, although he did not know that the Brahmin was Narayan in disguise. Drona has all his life investigated into the science of warfare and the use of arms. So it is likely that he will study it in relation to the other issues of life, at least it is necessary for him to know the moral and ethical sides of this science of his proved excellence. We know very often in the Mahabharata abstract truth is made palpably concrete through the use of myth, all the apparent incongruities of ideas and expressions are referred back to the central point of the concealed truth. One such incongruity is to be noted here too. Drona prayed for the boon of Narayanastra to a man whom he knew simply to be a Brahmin; why did he not think then if it was within his power to give such a rare thing ? Boon may be granted by anyone, but the nature of the boon must depend on the capacity of the giver, the suppliant ought to consider it if he wants his desire to be fulfilled. If in any way he does not consider it the boon-giver might only record his sanction by a wistful suggestion when it goes beyond his power. Everyday we note it in our sweet relationship with the superiors, this convention was not out of vogue completely in that mythical age, rather in different forms boon-giving was a common mode of exchage between intimate affectionate relations in those days. So Drona in his study of the military science was looking for the highest perfection of his weapons, and this preoccupation of his mind must have unconsciously come out when he was to opt for a boon. He asked for an invincible weapon and his desire was granted, not only in a patronizing gesture but in an actual fulfilment. The giver was in disguise Narayan himself. The highest attainments in Indian belief come from the gift of God. The God-given qualities in him made Drona a master of the science, in which again he attained the greatest possible perfection. Mythically the Brahmin wished him this attainment and he actually achieved it in his sole concentration on its cultivation, as if it had come from Narayan himself through the Lord's gift of inspiration and insight.

The weapon, when it is got in some such reasonable way, through such divine inspiration and illumination, as a divine gift, must have some moral and spiritual bearing upon its use and operation. Anything divine cannot stand neutral to the wider issues of life and justice. Hence we have an enunciation of principles to be observed by the possessor of this weapon, which comes from the mouth of the Brahmin in his quintessential entity of Lord Narayan :

Na tvidang sahasā Brahman prayoktabyang kathangchana,
Atha sankhye rathasyaiba shastrānāng cha bisarjanam,
Prayāchatāng cha shatrunām gamanang sharanasya cha.
Ete prashamane yogā mahāstrasya parangtapa,
Sarbathā pīrhito hi syādabadhyān pīrhayan rane.

(Ibid. 34-37)

The weapon, being an irresistible one, must not be used indiscriminately in escapable situations and on flimsy grounds; nor should it be inflicted upon soldiers laying down arms and abandoning their chariots, nor upon those retreating and entreating shelter or protection; its use in such cases would prove a boomerang to the user himself—thus the disguised Lord Narayana stipulated the moral principles of the weapon's use.

Asvathama narrated how his father got this invincible weapon and how he later inherited it from his father. He mentioned this weapon in particular with a moral disquisition upon its use because he was convinced that it was the proper occasion for its use, his father was killed in a trickily cruel battle in absolute disregard of all acknowledged rules of warfare. He felt this wrong was to be righted by the use of this unfailing sacred weapon.

Asvathama's determined stand brought about a complete turn of the situation. The Kaurava troops now took heart and consolidated their retreating ranks for a retaliatory assault upon the Pandava army. It was Yudhisthira who first noted the turn of the course of the war. He heard a heart-shaking roar at a distance in the Kaurava army indicating as it were the end of the world, repeated in quick succession to knonck all their hearts even after such a remarkable victory. Yudhisthira did not know who it was that made the sound. Now Arjuna explained to him the source of the sound and the terror that it caused. He knew it was Asvathama in his brimming vigour and rage that gave the call. It was he who at birth burst into terrific neighing cry of the divine horse Ucchaisbraba so that the three worlds quaked. Such a war-cry that struck terror into every heart could only be given by him. Then Arjuna who was aggrieved at the unusual cruelty of

Dhristadyumna in his act of killing his war-guide, Dronacharya, in a manner that shocked all and inflamed Asvathama to a terrible fury of war. He narrated how bitterly Asvathama took the ugly treatment of his father in war, Dhristadyumna did not care to show proper respect to the dead body of the noble hero, rather he savagely pulled at the locks of his head and severed the head itself when there was no sign of life in the body. Arjuna thought Asvathama would no longer spare the man who had done it. Such an ignominous death of his father rightly infuriated him.

(2)

Arjuna did not end there. He began to reproach his brother Yudhisthira for his most cowardly trick. He directly alleged that the most respected preceptor forsook arms only owing to the lie which he told him. It was, therefore, he who was responsible for his death. It was a double sin which he committed in this case. He wrongly exploited the preceptor's firm conviction in his honesty, he also could not shun all his pretension to piety, particularly in the manner of his telling the lie. Arjuna considered all these a gross sin.

Precisely Arjuna's role in this context is quite revealing of his character and his relationship with Drona. In the passage he did not end with his complaints in clear terms, he pointed out his deeply emotional relationship with his Guru. He said,

Abrīnīta sadā putrān māmebābhyadhikang Guruh,
Abekshamānstvāng māng cha nyastastrashchāhabe hatah.

* * * * * *

Putrān bhrātrrin pitrrin dārānjībitang chaiba bāsabih,
Tyajet sarbang mama premnā jānātyebang hi me Guruh.

(Ibid. Chap. 196, 47-8)

Dhritarastra named Bhisma and Drona with his sons in his testament for their share in the entire world under his control : in spite of that Drona my preceptor rated me more than his sons, but yet I had the heart to remain indifferent to his being slain in war in a state of absolute renunciation of arms. . . . my Guru had the profoundest confidence in me that I would surely shun my sons, brothers, parents, and wives and even my life for his sake—thus Arjuna lamented in self-accusation.

Even from a scrappy quotation from an elaborate monody it appears how deeply involved Arjuna was in his personal relationship with his Guru! His complete annoyance over the whole hoax-episode was only partly justified. From the exposition of the episode in the next preceding chapter it is to be noted that things did not occur as Arjuna alleged. Drona did not really die because he immediately relinquished arms at Yudhisthira's covert lie; the truth is Drona did not immediately do it. But Arjuna is quite correct to suggest that Yudhisthira acted in a grieveously sinful way to avoid sin. He held him solely responsible for the death of his beloved Guru, the manner of his death entirely won Arjuna's already softening heart. In his warmth of feeling Arjuna lost sight of the facts and the other side of the affair.

The side of the truth that was thus blurred in Arjuna's already disturbed vision did not escape the otherwise steady Bhima's notice. Bhima only cared for broad generalities of life, he had neither the kind of deep affection Arjuna had for his Guru, nor knew any thorough-going analysis of the delicate moral side of the issue. He got behind the question no further than the acknowledged outlines of human behaviour. He pointed out Arjuna's mistake. Arjuna in his over-emphasis of his personal relationship with Drona forgot his duty as a Kshatriya, he was then talking like an ascetic engaged in his personal purification course in the forest and like a Brahmin :

Muniryathāranyagato bhāsase dharmasanghitam,
Nyastodando yathā Pārtha brāhmanah sangshritabratah
Kshatatrātā kshatajjiban kshantā strīsvapi sādhusu,
Kshatriyah kshitimāpnoti kshipr ng dharmang yashah shriyah.

(Ibid. Chap. 197, 3-4)

He reminded Arjuna of the distinct character of a Kshatriya's Dharma, which constitutes in protecting from harm and injury all life of the righteous and the womenfolk.

Bhima, as I have already remarked in the earlier article, had at least the knowledge of the accepted norms of different class-divisions and their natural occupations. He had pointed it out with regard to the Brahmin like Drona earlier, and now he elaborated a Kshatriya's birth duty and the wrong that was done them by the Kaurava brothers under the nose of Drona and Bhisma. They not only deprived them of their share of the kingdom but also did the most savage act with regard to Draupadi : she was hauled up into the open court and disrobed in presence of these heroes, Bhima reminded Arjuna of all these wrongs and accused him of his infirmity and self-contradiction. His mind must have been hopelessly obsessed in his praise of Asvathama, ignoring any other more praiseworthy hero on their side, particularly Krishna. He must be rather ashamed to waste his compassion upon those who really did not deserve it. When thus Bhima ended Dhristadyumna rose to exculpate himself from the alleged wrongs.

Dhristadyumna, as we have remarked in the earlier article, was a special creation as it were for meeting Drona. He had no deep respect for a Guru who could fight indiscriminately against his disciples. In order to justify his acts and in refutation of Arjuna's charges, he gave his view of Dronacharya's mistaken role in all his life and in war. His first charge was that he was a Brahmin by birth, whose natural occupation he abandoned and took to a Kshatriya profession :

Apakrāntah svadharmāchcha kshātradharmang byapāshritah.
(Ibid. 26)

It is not only that he was at this old age recklessly killing whomsoever he met on the war front, but also that he made no distinction between right and wrong in rage, he blurred the distinction between Kshatriya and Brahmin, and made all-out attempts upon lives unknown to the use of such supra-sophisticated weapons (Brahmāstra) as he ruthlessly used. He also ignored all stipulated codes of military etiquette, and killed friends and relations from Panchal. Dhristadyumna thus supported his very grim acts of dealing with Drona.

Arjuna quite silently took all these counter charges of Dhristadyumna, his only response was a few long-drawn sighs and trickling drops of tears on end, it went so deep into his personal passion that justification in general terms was hardly possible. The other heroes on their side, including even Krishna, shamefacedly stood there without any comments of their own. Only

Satyaki rudely protested. He started with reproachful words, which Dhristadyumna would not accept. So it could ultimately turn to an armed conflict between the two heroes if only Lord Krishna did not timely intervene. Satyaki's objection was to the manner in which Dhristadyumna killed the honoured Guru, he allowed the fight, even he intervened (as may be noted in the earlier article) in the encounter to save him when he saw Drona use a weapon which he did not know how to fend off. But he could not accept the dishonour done to the respectable hero even after his death, it was too cruel for that.

They were locked in a shower of abuse, they explored their past and the crimes of their respective families, and then were about to engage in an armed duel. Just then Krishna intervened by sending Bhima to restrain them. They were restrained, and by that time the reorganized Kaurava army headed by Asvathama was seen in full battle array.

(3)

The above account will show how things had taken shape before Asvathama invoked that divine weapon called Narayanastra. The very invocation provoked the Nature in reaction, which paralleled a similar reaction among the embattled troops. Sanjay was narrating to Dhritarashtra how the whole nature was running counter to its normal course at the appearance of Narayanastra :

Prābāt saprisato bāyuranabhre stanayitnumān,
Chachāla prithibī chāpi chukshubhe cha mahododhih,
Pratisrotah prabrittāshcha gantung tatra samudragāh.

(Ibid. Chap. 196, 1-2)

There was thunder-clap in the cloudless sky, there were rain, and tempestuous wind, though the sky was clear; the earth was quaking, the oceans were angry, and the sea-going rivers turned their tides just in the opposite direction. This and many things else happened in nature as signs of a cataclysmic disturbance.

This, however, reminds one of modern nuclear warfare which goes so far as to poison the atmosphere and make nature play many an unwarranted prank.

The weapon rose first as a single rocket, then flew past over a distance to explode in the air into thousands of shapes and colours covering the enemy positions in ever expanding circles. Then emerged from it in thousands fire-tipped missiles like so many flamming adders, and in a moment showered rays spread across the sky, the horizon and the troops, and then appeared in millions the blazing bludgeons in heavens like countless diminutive luminaries, as also came club-shaped projectiles, two-wheeled and four-wheeled propellers, all burning like revolving and sweeping celestial bodies in space.

Prādurāsangstato bānā dīptāgrāh khe sahasrashah,
Pāndabān kshapayisyanto dīptāsyāh pannagā iba.
Te dishah khang cha sainyang cha samābrinvan mahāhabe,
Muhurtād bhāskarasyeba loke rājan gabhastaya.
Tathāpare dyotamānā jyotīngsībāmalāmvare,
Prādurāsan...kārsnāyasamaya gurhāh.
Chatushchakrā dvichakrāshcha shataghnyo bahulā gadāh
(Ibid. 199, 16-19)

This seems to be the forerunner of the modern ballistic missiles only kept within a limited range to hit a less remote target.

Asvathama charged this highly sophisticated weapon, and the Pandava army could not resist it, they sustained heavy casualties. Yudhisthira felt panicky and immediately ordered retreat and advised even Dhristadyumna to fight no more. He asked Satyaki to fall back and thought, regarding Krishna he had nothing to do, he would find out his own means of escape. He lost all hope of victory, rather thought that he would soon die with all his friends and relations. He lamented, although he had crossed the high seas successfully fighting out Bhisma and Drona, he would now have the sad luck of sinking in the puddles dying at the hands of a fry like Asvathama.

Lord Krishna watched him in this mourning mood and took the initiative to guide them. Yudhisthira only wished Krishna would arrange his own security, but he ought to know that Krishna did never think of his own safety alone. For the safety of the entire army he devised means and directed methods. He asked them to dismount their steeds and chariots and lay down arms and lie flat upon the ground wherever they stood and give up all thoughts of hostility from their minds. He told them the weapon would destroy where there would be resistance, and none escape its destructive blow with thoughts of war in his mind, even though he might hide himself in the nether world.

The whole army did as they were bidden, but there was only one exception, Bhima. He was a little more impulsive and exacerbated than his brothers. So he could not accept an apparently awkward stand. He forbade the troops to give up arms and fly their positions. He would lead them in war and by the strength of his arms protect them all. He assured them that he would resist the weapon if there be no other person to do it. Surely he was not a sufficient match for Narayanastra. Without caring for Krishna's warning he rushed towards Asvathama and launched a terrible attack with all sharp-hitting missiles at his disposal. At this useless agility of Bhima Asvathama only smiled and discharged a shower of projectiles towards him, which covered him from all sides and all over like so many sparks of gold and blazing serpents, so that he appeared to be a mountain at night bedecked with gleaming fireflies. The whole of the Pandava army stunned with fear shunned all their thoughts of war and their arms as Krishna asked them. The terrible weapon was seen aimed direct at the head of Bhima, and they raised a cry of horror.

Arjuna still stood indifferent to the course of war. He had already told Bhima that he would not take arms against cows, women and Brahmins. It is not that he gave up arms for Krishna's warning but that he was directed by his own sense of the right. But accidentally his course fell into line with Krishna's directives, so he was saved. All the other troops now willingly or out of fear acted upon Lord Krishna's advice. They were convinced how terrible the weapon could be, particularly from the scene of horror Asvathama's assault upon Bhima then created. Now the trouble was how to save Bhima who ignored Krishna's timely warning. Although Arjuna vowed he would not take arms against a Brahmin, he could not stand idle at the miserable plight of his brother. He launched his Barunastra (fire extinguishing weapon of water) to protect Bhima who was already burning with the flaming weapons all around him and was blazing as a mount of sulphur.

The neutralizing weapon now charged by Arjuna made an outer cover of mist round the girdle of fire as a sheet of cloud. It only hid Bhima from the sight of the army, Krishna knew it could not save him. In his desperate state his intervention was necessary. Lord Krishna took Arjuna with him to get his way into the whirl-blast of fire that surrounded Bhima, and dragged him from his chariot when he was gasping and breathing hot with rage and persuaded him with difficulty to give up arms, telling him that armed encounter would be of no avail.

The arms that kill everyone could not kill, however, Lord Krishna and Arjuna under his protection, but why? The text of the Mahabharata does not leave it unexplained. The killing fire of the weapon did not touch Krishna

Bigāhya tou subalinou māyayā ābishatāng tathā.
Nyastashastrou tata stou tu nādahat soastrajoanalah,
Bārunāstra prayogāchcha biryabatvāchcha Krishnayoh.
(Ibid. Chap. 200, 11-12)

because of the use of the counteracting weapon scattering water (Barunastra), because of their unusual strength and non-use of arms, and finally because of the illusion that was created, no doubt, by the very divine presence of the Lord himself.

Really the Lord is an illusion by himself. He knows the right way to deal with whatever exigencies might arise. With this complete knowledge of the cause and effect, the past, present and future of everything he knows the clue to life and security. When he uses it in its living form it appears like an illusion or Maya. This happened when Krishna took the secret way to save Bhima quite intoxicated in the use of sheer physical force or the force of weapons already outmoded in the face of a supremely sophisticated instrument of war. The war that was then being fought under the guidance of Lord Krishna was a war of Dharma against Adharma, of life against death, of good against evil. So Krishna was never in two minds about the right method of war, even though others might obscure it in their personal impulses. Narayanastra an instrument of the right, it could not be resisted by force or by war against it, Krishna knew it before anybody else. So he advised them peace and piety as a measure of security.

The Pandavas with their allies had committed a wrong, as we have remarked, not by getting rid of Drona, but by the cruel and gruesome method they adopted. Narayanastra was sure to operate as an instrument of reprisal of that wrong.

The weapon worked, but it could do no damage to the Pandava army, nor even to Bhima who was timely brought back to peace, and not at all to Lord Krishna who was an embodiment of the supreme good where both right and wrong merge into the highest possibility of life and evolution, nor to Arjuna either who then remained with him and acted, although accidentally, as he wished. Only Bhima was tormented by the weapon and could have been slain if he was not timely persuaded by Krishna to fight no more.

(4)

Bhima was still heaving like a python with blood-shot eyes, but as he disengaged himself the pyrotechnics of that terrible missile subsided. The whole nature returned to its normal courses; the sky was clear, the four corners of the earth enjoyed peace and the wind took its normal direction.

Now that the irresistible Narayanastra was countermined all that was still left in the Pandava army consolidated their position for an attack. The Kaurava army then poised for a counterblast. Duryodhana asked Asvathama to use Narayanastra again. But it is a weapon that neither could be revoked nor revived. When Asvathama related this nature of the weapon he revealed a great truth about it. The weapon is a part of nature that works without any care for individual conveniences, it represents a moral principle. You can use it where nature has her sanction, and there alone it is irresistible as the law of nature. Asvathama told Duryodhana that when revived to serve a personal exigency the weapon would destroy the user. It would not serve any personal need. An attempt to do so would be dangerous to who makes the attempt. Asvathama, therefore, used other arms now to resist the attack.

There was nothing exceptional in the fight that followed. It was a conventional encounter with arms of ordinary use. But there must have been some excess in Asvathama's retaliatory on-thrust as a similar excess in cruelty caused the appearance of that divine weapon. Like the cosmic order there is a moral order to rule the human affairs, which is a perfect balance or harmony disturbed only by anything incompatible or in excess. Such a disturbance must have been caused now by Asvathama's mad fury. He discharged missiles from the launching instrument to hit the enemies who opposed him now, but he hit ten times as many as would have been the proper number. Lord Krishna who never took arms against them but only guided them there for the good of all, although others might not know it. He hit even him and at a time when he advised peace to the Pandavas, their enemies, by which means he asked them to meet that irresistible weapon.

For some such excess committed by Asvathama, perhaps, Arjuna now took arms against him and did not think it proper to remain indifferent to the course of war as he did before. Even the dispassionate observer like Sanjay, who was reporting the progress of war to that sightless king Dhritarastra, wondered that Arjuna went against his preceptor's son and used rude language to him. Although Narayanastra could not be used, other conventional weapons stirred no such ethical sense in the mind of Asvathama : even today similar thing is found to occur : people may forbear to use the highly destructive nuclear weapon because it spares none, not even the user in its air-polluting poison-effusing capacity, particularly by its repeated use, but yet they can indiscriminately use their conventional weapons with no risk of their own harm. Asvathama perhaps thought like this with regard to the repeated use of that ancient version of the modern nuclear weapons. But in the use of the best among the conventional weapons he had no such moral scruples or material considerations. Arjuna must have been very much offended at his use of deadly weapons against all alike without any discrimination.

At this stage Asvathama's main target of attack was Arjuna, and Krishna in particular. He must have known that the failure of such an unfailing weapon as Narayanastra was due to Krishna, the strategy suggested by him. He would now hit Krishna and would spare none. He launched such fire-arms with the calculated manoeuvrability of their range as might hit both the ranks in the front and the rear, both visible and invisible :

Drounishchukopa Pārthāya Krishnāyacha bishesatah,
Debairapi sudurdharsamastramāgneyamādade,
Drishyādrishyāngiranānuddishyāchāryanandanah.
(Ibid. Chap. 201, 15-16)

The charged weapons, although could be kept within a limit in their destructive force, and at a safe distance from their own side, had terrible reaction within that limited area of operation. Even lower animals on land and in water were not spared, and the people who had nothing to do with war were destroyed or left in gasping sickness.

Surely Asvathama far exceeded the wrong done to his father; Arjuna felt it and to counteract the force of those arms chose such arms as could easily undo that sick effect. He used Brahmastra, the weapon which could remove all adverse effect against life and health. So the weapons which Arjuna now used brought back nature to its normal courses. Man and animal heaved a sigh of relief. The Pandava army could not see Arjuna and Krishna completely engulfed in the fire and smoke that Asvathama's arms released Now that the cloud of smoke and the blaze of fire were removed they saw them coming out of it to their great surprise.

Asvathama wondered how it could be that Krishna and Arjuna who were hit by that irresistible weapon remained not only alive but as fresh as ever! He could not account for the failure of this weapon, particularly as this happened in the trail of another sad failure of Narayanastra. He wanted to know the reason, he thought also that all those assurances about the sacred weapon were false :

Dhik dhik sarbamidang mithyā...
(Ibid. 47)

He now wanted some authority to ask the reason, he got such an authority in Veda Vyas. While he was thus out of frustration leaving the field he met Vyas and asked why his arms failed to kill Krishna and Arjuna, although they could destroy other ranks of the enemy army. Vyas Deva narrated in this connection the previous births of those three, particularly of

Krishna. Asvathama learnt the science of arms from his father, but he did not know that Lord Krishna was the incarnation of the Omnipotent God. The all-knowing Rishi let him also know that even though the Creator of everything he was well within the cosmic order, all the virtues, even the supreme excellence, were of natural evolution in him, the highest state of all human qualities well-embodied in his human form. He was, therefore, Narayana, the ideal of attainments for mankind—both the way and the goal of life in one. So the Rishi gave an elaborate description of how Krishna attained that state of indestructibility, even by such unfailing weapons as the Narayanastra. I am, of course, not going to reproduce that long passage.

It is also a sure evidence which the Rishi cites here that man, too, can attain that indestructibility. The case in point is Arjuna. Arjuna is not Narayana, but Nara. But he is, too, beyond the scope of that weapon when in close company with Narayana. Whatever faults he may have in his life, he is safe when he can leave them behind him to follow the path of God, which is the real path of life, in every act and thought. Arjuna has now got that path and its goal in the form of the Lord's human incarnation. The Rishi then pointed out Lord Krishna as the supreme security of all life and the living.

Ebamete barā labdhāh purastād biddhi shourinā,
Sa esa debashcharati māyayā mohayanjagat.

(Ibid. 85)

Vyas Deva represents Lord Krishna as deriving a boon from Mahadeva who said that by his boon Krishna called Narayana, would be even more powerful than himself (*Mamādhikah*). It is also a part of the Mahabharata technique to use forecast to anticipate the future prospect of things as a matter of course. The boon episode symbolizes only what is in the heart of Nature herself. It is the highest gift of nature that the unmistakable way to perfection for mankind incarnates itself into a human form; the unlimited, the infinite, is measured up into a physical limitation; hence the cause of human misgivings as if from an illusion. The Rishi lets him know that Narayana is more powerful than Narayanastra, the weapon being only his gift to mankind; and that it works only when there is hostility to his eternal principle and not against those who are with him and on his path. Asvathama forgot it or did not know it as he did not know, or knew only when Vyas Deva explained to him, that Krishna was Narayana himself.

THE INVINCIBLE WEAPON CALLED VAISNABASTRA

There can be a good study of mythical weaponry from the greatest epic of the world in exploration of the ethical side of the science of warfare in the long past. The article is an attempt towards that end, of course in an isolated fragmentary form.

(1)

It is a fight between the two great heroes, Arjuna and Bhagadatta, that ultimately made the use of the invincible weapon called Vaisnabastra unavoidable. Krishna's role here is very significant. He vowed he would not take arms, or directly participate in the war of Kurukshetra, his work would be confined to guiding the course of Arjuna's chariot. But in one case he departed from his pledge. That was the subject of Arjuna's inquiry.

Bhagadatta charged all sorts of missiles at the two heroes, Krishna and Arjuna, to bring an end to their life, but all his efforts came to naught. He was in a rage to see that, and more so when Arjuna urged him slightingly even for a quick survey of all his near and dear ones who could be there in the hair's breadth gap of a moment before sure death. So he decided to discharge the most unfailing weapon in store to hit them. This is Vaisnabastra which he chose for a fateful missile. Vaisnabastra is a weapon which is required to be sanctified with sacred hymns before it could be discharged. Bhagadatta did it to make the weapon endowed with infinite force of destruction.

The missile was aimed at the heart of Arjuna, who could not, of course, anticipate the danger involved in it. So he took exception to what Krishna did to forestall its effect. Krishna took upon himself the fatal consequence of the missile. He stepped ahead of Arjuna to ward it off and keep him clear of sure death. Krishna shielded him with the whole span of his body, to receive it into his heart. Definitely it is in contravention of Lord Krishna's pledge of neutrality in war. Arjuna prayed him, therefore, kindly to explain the reason. Krishna assured him he would not take part in the actual conflict, but drive and control the horses of his chariot as guide in the field of war. He went back upon his word, and intervened in the actual fight. As soon as Krishna offered to receive the below of the invincible weapon into his heart the flint of the missile itself was transformed into Vaijaiyanti-Mala—a garland of absolute victory—upon the Lord's breast, a rare emblem of beauty ablaze with all the choicest leaves and petals of lotus and Palash, as though flaming with the glow of the moon; the myrtled leaves of incomparable grace, just leapt into life with a thrill of fresh-blowing breeze, lay there in the superb splendour of its glory :

Baijayantyabhabanmālā tadastrang Keshaborasi,
Padmakoshabichitrādhyā sarbartukusumotkatā.
Jvalanārkendubarnābhā pābakojjvalapallabā,
Tayā padmapalāshinyā bātakampita patrayā.
(Drona Praba, Chap. 29, 19-20)

This sort of trans-substantiation of a weapon into a thing of beauty struck Arjuna with wonder, which at last broke into a question : 'You have vowed not to use arms in the war, Lord, not to take part in it except as charioteer, why then left it not for me to deal with, well-armed and well-educated in the science of warfare and competent enough as I am ?' Arjuna thought his good name as a soldier compromised by Krishna's undue intervention in the conflict. Why should he resist the missile and shield him behind his back ? Could he not meet it himself ? With his supply of war instruments like the missile and the charging device he was equal to meeting gods and demons and the three worlds combined together.

Arjuna saw what was only apparent and estimated things only materially having no insight into its abtruse spiritual bearings. So Krishna hastened to explain his act. He narrated the history of the weapon, how it came to be in his possession in the course of time. He practically related his own divine roles in the cycles of Time and Creation. He addressed Arjuna to note how for the good of mankind and their salvation his divine being he divided into four forms. In one the Lord does his spiritual penance on earth, in the second he observes the good and evil acts of the whole universe, in the next he does all human deeds in this world assuming a human body, in the fourth stage of evolution he spends thousands of years in total inaction in a sort of sleep. When awakened to the spirit of action again from that absolute withdrawal the Lord pleased to distribute boons to those who took the chance of his awakened state by merits, of course. The words of the Mahabharata are of particular note :

Yāsau barsasahasrānte murtiruttistate mama,
Barārebhya barāng shrestāng stasmin kāle dadāti sā.
(Ibid. 29)

Lord Krishna did not say he distributed boons, but stated that the assumed form, the revealed embodiment, granted them not to all but to those alone who deserved them (*barārhebhyah*). Such a worthy suppliant was the Earth at such a break of Krishna's entranced state of complete indifference. The Earth did not ask that boon for her own sake, she asked it for her son, here Narakasura by name. She timed the prayer with the Lord's coming to a conscious state, to a particular frame of mind for human good :

Tang tu kālamanuprāptang biditva Prithibī tadā,
Ayāchata barang yanmāng Narakārthāya tachchhrinu.
(Ibid. 30)

The Earth-mother prayed for her son to Krishna that he should obtain as a boon the weapon of Vaisnabastra to be unslain by both gods and demons in war. Krishna granted that boon, saying 'Let this weapon be irresistible in war for the protection of Naraka, let none kill him for the sake of this possession and let your son grow unconquerably armed with it in all the world.'

(2)

There must have been a threat to the security of the Earth-born Naraka from all sides, that would have prompted the mother to seek Krishna's boon. She got it and returned well-content. Naraka too was safe with that weapon in spite of the menace. The lord of Pragjyotish came into possession of this weapon by descent and none in this universe was impregnable to this weapon, not even the Indra and the Rudra. Krishna narrated this history of the weapon; there was none to resist the force of this invincible missile, so Krishna took it upon himself to intervene in contravention of his pledge. Now he asked Arjuna to kill Bhagadatta himself just free from the menace of the unfailing weapon. He once extirpated Naraka for the good of all, so also Arjuna must kill the desperate enemy of the gods :

Bairinang jahi durdharsang Bhagadattang suradvisang,
Yathāhang jagnibān purbang hitārthang Narakang tathā.

(Ibid. 28)

Really speaking Krishna has explained the basis of his sanction and withdrawal of his favour, and the reason for the possessor of Vaisnabastra's immediate death. Krishna granted boon to the Earth who prayed him to ensure her son's security from possible oppression. His awakened state is really minding the divine mission of protective safeguard for all who require it. He does it in his revealed human form, which is sure to be explained as his awakened state. He would grant boon not to encourage cruelty or oppression, he must have given Naraka that weapon not for that; Naraka surely forgot it and used it for power and undue advantage, thus calling for Krishna's direct action to put an end to that sprouting root. This time Bhagadatta has taken a similar move like his father. He was tempted to use the sacred weapon not for his personal security, nor as a strategic deterrent, more for a psychological safeguard, like the modern nuclear weapons, but for cruel massacre of lives, for mere satisfaction of a sense of power. Bhagadatta took the side of evil when he decided to fight against the already persecuted Pandavas. He must have known how Krishna's mission of peace failed because of the power-puffed insolence of Duryodhana, how secretly the political caucus of Duryodhana's friends was planning all the miseries of the peace-loving Pandava brothers, to the extent of their secret murder and outrage upon their wife. Knowing all these Bhagadatta sided with the power-loving wicked tormentors, he threw missiles at Krishna too, who not only granted that boon of the cherished weapon now in his possession but also was vowed to neutrality in active war, and only undertook to guide the horses of the chariot on the side of Dharma. Bhagadatta did not spare even that pledged leader of peace, he was indiscriminately showering arms upon everything and everyone contrary to all rules of war. Times without number he aimed his missiles at Krishna not only to cripple his capability as charioteer but to take his life to be sure. His movements in the field of war are indicative enough that he went against the acknowledged principles of Dharma, and showed that he was carried into the path of active evil only through an illusion of strategic advantage in the fight.

The weapon that was orginally a gift of Lord Krishna in his human revelation for purely personal security of the possessor and the good of all others around him, reached him in its completely transformed state, it became a decoration, an article of beauty at the touch of his divine body. It is no wonder that it would be so. This weapon was initially a token of love, the Lord would not see his devotees unnecessarily tormented in their path of virtue. It is, therefore, love in another form, so it returned, when it had to, as an article of worship. It is quite significant that Lord Krishna received the blow upon the centre of his heart, because there it offended. The instrument of war is a symbol of his love, his earnest appeal to all seekers of life and tacit denial of oppression and death. Even the instrument of destruction stemmed out of the all-protecting melting soul of the Lord, hardened only against the dreaded enemies of life and truth. So when it returned, it came lithe and lambent as a suppliant in the blooming sense of relief, from a cruel oppressor.

(3)

Arjuna took the clue and began showering missiles one after another upon his insolent enemy. He hit first the carrier beast of Bhagadatta, as a war-trick perhaps, then released a weapon to hit Bhagadatta himself, now relieved of all his support.

The Creator's gift of a weapon cannot be calculated to encourage cruelty, in the epic it has not been, if one is ready to get behind the myth in the right frame of mind. The Lord's granted boon was not meant for all, we have seen, then it was granted to the mother Earth for the security of her son, which could be handed down to the generation coming after him, as it has been here. God wished security for all, and would see none in dread of death if he did not forfeit it by his own doings, by the invidious ill-will for another's life, or by posing a universal threat to life and security. In such a baneful misuse of God's gifts there must be a vehement reaction against it, which is life's reaction against death. Life's accommodation of all adverse and hostile situations for unbroken continuity and progress here is a truth of creation and an essential nature of life itself. The Lord of creation is the supreme embodiment of Life's true essence, the origin of all origins. In all his diverse roles, latent or potent, in his human form or otherwise, he serves the best purpose of life and its evolution, either in his act of creation, revitalization of all in their depleting stage, or even in the apparent act of destruction of inimical forces in an attempt to reorganize everything into the right order of mutual cooperation and co-existence. It is in Nature that the success or failure of this weapon lies. The name that is given to it is quite suggestive of it. Vishnu is the incarnation of the Creator in his protective role of created things, he creates for his own pleasure, but protects with a sense of responsibility, with love awakened to a sense of all good : so the weapon that he can grant for human good should serve this purpose, the name itself is a reminder to the possessor. Obviously it fails where the original purpose is defeated. It is in the nature of the instrument itself. So when Krishna acts as an interceptor of the missile aimed at undeserved targets he does it not in violation of his vow, but just in fulfilment of the principle embodied in and ordained by his essential being. He is the best and the completest repository of Nature (Prakriti), he being her all-nourishing all-fulfilling source (Purusa). The Purusa-Prakriti inseparable link is thus a myth of the Creation and its whole purpose.

Bhagadatta's days were numbered as earlier Naraka's were. Naraka's by the hand of Lord Krishna, and Bhagadatta's through the agency of Arjuna, it matters little who killed whom; they sinned against Nature and directly went against the true principle of life. They embraced evil and turned enemies to the gods and the good. It is the nature of the Creator to grant everyone his own free will, it is nature itself, while leaving yet a choice between the principles of life and their opposite. Whatever the ultimate choice it cannot escape the ulterior end. To Bhagadatta is meted out the end his chosen course deserved. The Lord is still in his neutral position. He is the true embodiment of Dharma, the principle that upholds and sustains life all through its ups and downs, rise and fall, expansion and contraction, through a sort of undulation that represents a march ahead.

Vaisnabastra illustrates the ethics of war, which is again a demonstration of the vital force that by nature seeks to survive all throes and assaults of annihilation. That is why the war that is fought in the Mahabharata is described as the war of Dharma, *i.e.* war of life against the aggression of death, and the field of battle as Dharma-Kshetra, where the war of life is fought. So the instrument of war has a peculiarity just consistent with the principle itself. It has the easiest way of transformation form an instrument of war to an article of worship. It has been as hard as flint, again has gone as soft as the gracefulness of a flower. The weapon is an emblem, as it were, of the eternal principle of life, of its natural evolution, rude to the enemy round the corner, but friendly, even softly suppliant to every move towards fulfilment and perfection, the assigned goal of life.

THE SACRIFICE THAT DAKSHA DID

The Mahabharata episode of Daksha's sacrifice is a common knowledge among the Indians, the article deals with that story only to put a plausible construction upon it so that one does not lose sight of its realistic basis in the overgrowths of myth.

(1)

Yudhisthira asked Grandfather Bhisma on his death-bed about some eternal truths one must know to be on the path of virtue. Story after story cropped up in the process of narration, one leading to the other for the sake of clarification of the link between the one point of reference and that of another, the usual method of epic inculcation. Yudhisthira passed from subject to subject in his inquiry into the secrets of life. He enquired about the work of Jvara (infirmity) in the ultimate destruction of Britta, an invincible demon. This led to the question of the origin of all infirmities affecting life, which again raised the issue how Mahadeva once sought to spoil Daksha's sacrifice by means of an irresistible power of total ruin born of his very wrath.

His father-in-law Daksha was once arranging a great sacrifice, to which all the three worlds were invited. By Mahadeva's leave all the Rishis and gods were in preparedness to attend it, when something untoward occurred to change his mind. Parbati his divine consort felt extremely pained at the neglect of her all-powerful Lord, her father extended invitation to all grades of gods and Rishis, but withheld it from the God of all gods, Mahadeva. Parbati complained to her Lord why was he grudged that formal invitation? It matters very little whether Daksha sent him invitation or not, he was too self-absorbed and too indifferent for that. He explained to his spouse that in the original conception of Jajna he was not assigned any share; this explanation was in a sense an eyewash, designed for the satisfaction of his darling bride. But Parbati would not accept it for explanation, her father had not done right, she would not swallow it. It became a question of self-respect to her, her Lord would not be invited to a grand sacrifice at her father's capital where all the gods were accosted!

Mahadeva could have ignored it but for Parbati, his consort. She said openly she could not accept that primordial proposition depriving the greatest god of his share of his sacrificial beatitude. Mahadeva understood the sore point of her argument and left Nandi there when himself went straight to visit the sacrificial place sweating in rage of slighted self-respect. With the help of his other devilish accomplices in his retinue spoiled the whole arrangement for sacrifice. Even Jajna the god fled in the shape of a deer whom he pierced with his trident. It is mythologically represented that while chasing that fleeing deer Shiva shed drops of perspiration from his brow burning with ire and annoyance, which caught fire upon the ground and gave birth to a terrific form of jet black complexion, death and destruction in their sole human form as it were. Born of extreme disgust and wrath that dwarfish deadly-looking shaggy demon burnt the deer-shaped Jajna and turned to the assembly of gods and Rishis, who in gasping fear fled the sacrificial ground to seek shelter where they could. The whole earth was quaking under his feet. This is Jvara infirmity, born for the destruction of all.

The great creator Brahma, seeing the new force of destruction, approached Mahadeva seeking to restrain its destructive power, and told him that the gods would henceforth apportion his part of the sacrifice. Then he enjoined appealing 'the hero born of

Yashchaisa puruso jātah svedāt te bibhudhottama,
Jvaro nāmaisa dharmajna lokesu pracharisyati.
Ekibhūtasya na tvasya dhārane tejasah prabho,
Samarthā sakalā prithvī bahudhā srijyatāmyam.

(Santi Parba, Chap. 283, 47-48)

your sweat, you the best of the Lords, would be called Jvara and would haunt the world : but divide it into many parts as the whole world would not bear the force of its united impact.'

This the best of the gods Mahadeva did. He divided it into innumerable bits for the affliction of different creatures in different ways in their reduced force. However interesting that elaborate distribution of infirmity in the text of the epic, let us foreshorten it for a still more interesting account thereof.

The Jvara was born ultimately of Shiva's wrath and annoyance, sweat was only its immediate cause; and it was caused for the destruction of Daksha's sacrifice and impelled by Parbati's mourning appeal, a mythical truth. The further secret of the story comes out from the detailed account of it, which Yudhisthira later curiously asked of their grandfather Bhisma.

(2)

In the detailed account there are some new modifications, which reveal the truth behind the mythical apparatus. The Rishis, when they reached the sacrificial ground, saw that the all-worshipful Mahadeva was not invited there. This grievious wrong was pointed out publicly by Rishi Dadhichi. 'The sacrifice where Rudra is not invited and honoured cannot bring forth any good, nor can it be of any merit. I see the ruin and captivity of all who are present here,' the Rishi warned. Then he saw in his tranced state Rishi Narada worshipping Mahadeva and Parbati at their Himalayan seat. He sensed the impending peril out of this glaring omission. So the assembled gods and Rishis withdrew in a secret conclave where Dadhichi forewarned Mahadeva's fateful appearance there.

Perhaps thus warned by the spokesman of the joint assembly of gods and Rishis, Daksha may have sought to support his step pleading his lack of knowledge of Mahadeva's position among the eleven Rudras; at which Dadhichi retorted, 'You have unilaterally decided not to invite Mahadeva, that is the truth; but you must know that there is none among us gods greater than he, and this omission will surely lead to the complete spoilage of your sacrifice.'

Daksha retorted in reply that he had reserved in the gold receptacle the share of Vishnu in the sacrifice, the milk-cream sanctified with the hymn of God (Mantra), by which the Lord would be invoked.

This Daksha did and said really to escape censure. Parbati, however, in her crucial position between father and husband, took upon herself the entire responsibility for undoing the obstacle in the way of her Lord's obtaining the second or third share of the sacrifice. She thought to herself what kind of vow or penance or charity on her part could ensure her Lord's share :

King nāma dānang niyamang tapo bā,
Kuryāmahang yena patirmamādya,
Labheta bhāgang bhagabānachintyo
Hyardhang tathā bhāgamatho tritīyam.

(Ibid. Chap. 284, 22)

Mahadeva had explained his position to his consort and done something to appease his divine spouse, as in the text of the Mahabharata; but this time further elaboration comes and quite significantly.

Mahadeva now humoured his chagrined leman by saying, 'Darling, you do not know how to speak of me, none without deep meditation can know me, by your misconception all the three worlds and Indra with his cohort of gods are getting dazed; the hymn-reciters sing in praise of me in the sacrifice, the Brahmins with the sacred rhymes from the Sam Veda sing of me, the Brahmins with their knowledge of the Prime cause worship me and the priests apportion the share of the sacrifice to me'.

When Mahadeva disclosed the secret regarding his own share of the sacrifice Parbati took it otherwise. His idea was whether Daksha his father-in-law reserved his share or not the ritualist priests and Brahmins would, of course, in their conduct of that grand sacrifice, hymn it to him, the god of gods. But Parbati mistook it for self-praise which, she thought, even a mean creature would adopt in presence of women :

Suprākritoapi purusah sarbah strijanasangsadi,
Stouti garbāyate chāpi svamātmānang na sangshayah.

(Ibid. 27)

The text of the epic tells us here, Mahadeva made a modest protest to what Parbati said slightingly that he was not of the nature of self-adulation. So not exactly of his own accord but simply out of an annoyed repulsed state of mind he produced something to satisfy Uma, his spouse. This time the text differs from the earlier account. Mahadeva created a terrible hero not from his temple but from his mouth, and he was not called Jvara now, but Birbhadra. There came forward another female form too of the name of Mahakali. Mahadeva asked that hero to immediately destroy Daksha's sacrifice in order to soothe Parbati's anger, and the female form who then came into being was born of that anger. And in pursuit of her true part that great embodiment of terror of a woman followed him in that act of destruction :

Manyunācha mahābhīmā mahākāli maheshvarī.
Ātmanah karmasākshitve tena sārdhang sahānugā,
(Ibid. 31-32)

The apparent discrepancy and difference between the two versions of the same episode in the same epic are not altogether unaccountable. This is in the very nature of the mythological style, which pays less attention to the details than to the essential truth and spirit. It is a style that aims at the grain of truth rather than the coat which might often serve as a well-calculated veneer. So the variation although striking has not eventually disturbed the truth, rather helped comprehension.

The relation between the divine consorts under the impact of the father-in-law's gratuitous insult entered a phase of secret distrust and reservation, which came out only partly in notched-up language. From the disregard shown to him by her father, Parbati must have suspected Siva's elevated position among the whole lot of gods, she took Siva's self-praise for an empty vaunt which male creatures often utilize as a trick to tempt women-folk. Although the great Lord of the gods talked humouringly he may have felt an inward disgust so terrible for its being kept carefully under the false attitude of apparent affection that it caused even physical fatigue in the Lord, which may have been conveyed through a symbol of collected sweat upon his forehead. The same earlier symbol does not seem quite incompatible with the later interpretation of the birth of two pestilential creatures, Birbhadra and Mahakali for a joint adventure of destruction. Jvara and the latter two destructive embodiments born one of Siva the other of the ire of Parvati.

The thing is, the whole destructive and pestilential force sprang from an unholy, chagrined and secretly strained relationship between the hereto loved consorts. From this psycho-physical state all distempers are born, such hidden reservation in conjugal relationship is at the root of all diseases, so it is Jvara the secret source of all diseases, (leader of all diseases—Monier). When the Primal father and mother were seized with the secret distemper over apparently a very flimsy cause, their union gave birth to a universal plague. Birbhadra and Mahakali were the incidental outcome of that state of Jvara first affecting their minds, mainly the mind of the father who adversely reacted to that attitude of subdued disrespect and neglect from the loved one, so the sweat collected symptomatically upon his brow. From their physical union, which might have been inevitable from their attempt to maintain an unruffled outward facade, naturally brought forth the twin destructive embodiments of the names already known. Mahadeva, who knew what their strained relationship would come to, ironically told his spouse what havoc their issues would wreak upon the sacrifice of her father. Mahadeva knew the result, but could not restrict its effect. So the evil; which came down into their issues from their bitter-sweet kind of conjugal relation, caused fear even to the outside world. Out of Birbhadra's being were born a host of evil creatures, as if from every pore of his body, every one as terrific as the Rudra himself. Their first target was the destruction of Daksha's sacrifice, but the horrid howl and yell that they set up struck terror into the heat of everything and every one in the three worlds.

The destruction of this terror-tense atmosphere in the epic has all the mythical grandeur. I do not quote the extract, it is long, but bring out the sense of it. The evil of distorted conjugal relation gives rise to a train of evil even in the successive generations if they are not otherwise counteracted by scientific methods of eugenic and matrimonial manipulation. The universality of its application is not disturbed even in respect of gods and goddesses. Mahadeva, being the foremost of the gods, knew it and forewarned the advent of mighty evil from their union.

(3)

To come back to the story the two, brother and sister, born of the union of Siva and Parvati made a mess of Daksha's sacrifice with all their wild legion. Daksha could not at first know who they were. He along with all the leading gods prayed to them with folded palms enquiring their personal names and connections. Birbhadra rejoined for them two that he was neither Lord Rudra nor she the goddess Parbati, nor had he appeared there to enjoy the rituals of the sacrifice. He told Daksha how he had the companion woman character born. This is one step closer to the realistic basis of their origin.

Bīrabhadra itikhyāto Rudrakopāt binihsritah.
Bhadrakālīti bikhyātā debyāh kopāt binihsritā,

(Ibid. 53-54)

They were born one of the ire of Rudra, the other of the wrath of the goddess, just a mythical style of communication. The truth behind it is, they were born of the secret repugnant reservation which disturbed the healthy urge that should have characterized their union, giving rise to the twin-born brother and sister. So they were not for any good, they were for mischief, they appeared there to bring an end to the sacrifice. He, of course, helped him with a remedy.

Sharanang gachchha biprendra debadebamumāpatim.

(Ibid. 55)

'Go into complete surrender to the God of all gods, that Lord of goddess, Uma, thou foremost of the Brahmins'. Birbhadra asked him to do it to put right what went wrong. Daksha took this advice and assured him that he would propitiate that Almighty Lord. He then started chanting hymn to Mahadeva. Mahadeva could have remained indifferent to the invitation to Daksha's sacrifice or any claim of share in it. His ire arose by his wife's annoyance and covert insinuation to his worth. So when Daksha came to worship that Lord who had the nature of easy self-content, the whole thing managed to mend itself. Mahadeva arose from the whirl of fire—*Agnikundāt samutthitah*—a well-content changed god. It is really the transformed state of the god's volatile mood, a favourable transformation from ire to appeasement; and that was made possible by the changed attitude of Daksha who performed the sacrifice for the good of his own and the world. That is really the highest object of all divine rites and rituals. The success of a Jajna as it was called in ancient India depends not merely upon the material supplies but mainly upon the mood with which the rites are observed : Daksha had no lack of material supply, rather provided more than there was need, but he lacked the proper mood that could produce good of his own and the world at large. He had no broadness of mind, no love for the world, no spirit of tolerance. He could not extend invitation to his own son-in-law who happened to be the god of all good—Siva. He thought him ugly and naked, his presence in his pompous court, he may have thought quite offensive to taste and decorum. His ungenerous snobbish motive alienated one of his near relations from the joy and benefit of the sacrifice; the man who is thus deprived of the share of good of the sacrifice which ought to have been extended to all is eventually the emblem of the highest good. Even the gratuitous injury to his self-respect, a wilful offence to his official position among the gods could not normally turn him to a hostile attitude : he could remain indifferent to it, because he was too self-absorbed in contemplation of the highest good of the Universe; that is why he was called Siva, the source of all good.

Denying share of the benefit of a grand sacrifice to a god of this stature and attitude Daksha has practically incurred the wrath of Nature, an adverse reaction from his own blood, his daughter Parbati. Mahadeva acted under the repulsed and chagrined prompting of his beloved spouse, not exactly of his own, as we have seen. Daksha is paid in his own coin, his danger came from the unexpected corner, from the children of his own daughter, from the daughter herself although she may not have meant it to that extent. Daksha's diseased mentality, its uncharitable narrowness infected not too remotely the eugenic principle of his own blood directiy to his own evil.

Daksha must have been taught this ethical lesson through a complex yet attractive mythical grandeur. He is taught also how to undo the already snaring evil effect of his parochial outlook. He came to his senses to detect his own folly. So he forgot his abhorence of the queer and uncouch manners and ways of his son-in-law and got over the reservation he had against his daughter's ungainly union with, in his view, an unmajestic unkempt god—a marriage, as it were, between a princess and a beggar. He failed to appreciate the inner worth of the god, and was guided perhaps by the wrong idea of the surface gloss and attractive costume of the person to be selected for his daughter, and took no notice of his daughter's mind and choice, which was against the true concept of marriage. He wanted to act as an oppressive father perhaps conceding no right of choice to his daughter. It is wrong to allow no free choice of a daughter when she can do it rightly and with the full support of her mind and heart and under no obsessing prompting of any other kind. The father's duty would be to stand guard against any possible wrong selection under any seductive inducement. Daksha ha s not done it here, but only wanted to assert his authority mainly under the notion of an imposing status in the matter of his daughter's marriage, the status of the groom.

In the text of the epic there is no explicit account of the reasons why Daksha withheld invitation from his son-in-law, it is only stated that he did not know which of the eleven Rudras his son-in-law was, and pretended having reserved in the golden vessel the sanctified milk-cream for Vishnu as if this would satisfy Mahadeva too. This last pretence seems to be a trick to avoid Mahadeva, one of the Trinity. However reticent about the strained relation between the in-laws, the reserved attitude of the father is effectively conveyed through the half-articulate and half-subdued style of the mythical interpretation.

Now soon after the broil Daksha came to his senses and reformed his outlook to know the true purpose and object of his sacrifice. He softened his attitude to his daughter's selection, which was no wrong choice but only misjudged by his obsessed mind to be so. He knew the essential greatness of the god deceptive in appearance and indifferent by nature. The god too came to be content with the restored good relation. He asked Daksha to have a boon after his own choice.

We know in the mythological scheme every boon is not a mere windfall but well-deserved by force of quite a changed attitude and a conducive mental and spiritual realignment. It is a stylistic device to focus on a moral and spiritual turning-point for the better. So it comes here when Daksha asks a boon for the success of his sacrifice which was spoiled by the descendants from his own daughter. It is very significant that Daksha should ask for a boon like that :

Churnīkritāpabiddhang cha yajnasambharamidrisham.
Dirghakālena mahatā prayatnena susangchitam,
Tanna mithyā bhabenmahyang barametamahang brine.
(Ibid. 63-64)

'Lord, let them not go without merit, the sacrificial materials which I have been accumulating for long years with perfect care, all that have been either broken or bestrewn; grant me this boon.'

Mahadeva granted it intently. Daksha attained already the state of mind, the moral and spiritual outlook of love and forbearance that normally make sacrifice a success. Boon is granted at a time when it is deserved by virtue of spiritual attainment, and the nature of the boon is conditioned by one's desert. Whether one asks it or given without asking, a boon would be in the right proportion to what one may merit by one's spiritual worth. Here the sanction is the success of the sacrifice itself which Daksha asked and Mahadeva allowed willingly. Everything is in a law of cause and effect sequence, in an inviolable moral and spiritual order. Boon and bane are the two opposite extremes of reaction in that order. A god's offer or boon is a symptomatic expression of the merit of a deserved case. Daksha received the boon he deserved by a change of his moral outlook.

CREATOR WHO CREATES DEATH TOO

In this article an attempt is made to probe the mystery of Death, a piece of myth in the treatment of the Mahabharata. In this analysis the side of myth and its realistic implication, both are taken into consideration, and both taken together reveal the uniqueness of this episode and make it a magnificent piece of literature.

(1)

In the battle of Kurukshetra a large number of indomitable heroes died, and died also that invincible boy Abhimanyu in an irregular fight : Yudhisthira was inconsolably pained at heart at the death of the latter in particular and the irresistible nature of death itself. It seemed to him a mystery which he sought to know from that sage Veda Vyas who was famed for his knowledge of the past, present and future of things. What is death, how came it to be, and why does it bring to an end all that is created ?—Yudhisthira wanted to know.

For the consolation of king Yudhisthira Vyas narrated what he knew the great sage Narada had earlier told about it in a similar situation. The Mahabharata, as we all know, has the technique of interweaving story within story very often. Narada related the story of death to remove the soul-sinking grief of king Akampana at the loss of his well-accomplished son Hari by name.

Brahma, the ultimate source of the Universe and all the worlds that have been, created life and did not then think of the problem of the ever-swelling numbers. He confronts this problem now that the earth is ever-burdened with life and its unending and undiminished march ever since. The earth is too full of the trailing generations, it cannot hold any more unless the present set makes room for the future. Now the creator is thinking out any solution that can be, and the result is the creation of Death. But Death did not come into existence in so simple a process as it seems. The myth of her origin in the Mahabharata has all the charm of a fairy tale on the one hand and the true nature of the creative process on the other.

Brahma saw at long last that none in his creation was dying, but daily a new life was being born on the already over-populated earth. His excited worry took on the form of wrath which gave birth to the all-consuming fire. This fire was then doing its work, threatening the total destruction of everything in heaven, earth and hades. At the sight of this universal annihilation without any discrimination, Mahadeva (described here as Sthanu—'well-composed') became full of compassion and appeared before the Grandfather of the whole creation as Brahma is called because of his being the ultimate source of life of all lives. Sthanu, who is also Rudra the terrible in one of his changed roles, was then affectionately received by that great father, having been addressed as his darling son born of his desire :

King kurmah kāmang kāmārha kāmājjātoasi putraka

(Drona Parba, Chap. 52, 45)

Sthanu then explained to the well-disposed Father the purpose of his untimely appearance. He could not bear to see the whole creation thus perish by the fire of his father's wrath. He knew Brahma did not create this Universe for that, then how came it so to turn his mind against life ? Brahma gave his reason saying—

Prithibyā hitakāmang tu tato māng manyurābishat

(Ibid. Chap, 53, 3)

He has done it for the benefit of the earth, she is tormented by the undiminished pressure of population. The text has *Bhārārtā bhārenābhihatā* epithets applied to the earth.

Then Creator the Son, Siva (of course this word is not used here) implored the Father to forbear and recall the fire of total annihilation, he begged him that boon. He also explained to him the consequence of this unlimited and uncontrolled scheme of destruction : it is a long passage, so I am not going to quote it. The essence of his plea for a changed mood in Creator the Father is that it will lead to the end of all life without any exception, branding his creation itself as a mere useless freak.

Brahma understood his plea for controlled anger and for limited destruction. He saw it would rather suit his purpose. He then strained all his nerves and sense organs to restrain the already inflamed anger within him. In trying to do so he felt that unlimited fire of destruction reduced to a limited force called death just emerging from his body in the terrible form of the beauty of a lady. It is thus that death first made its appearance in the scheme of creation.

(2)

Brahma now enjoins Death to destroy life, because she has been born of his destructive impulses; he assures too that she will have her own good out of it :

Mrityo iti mahīpāla jahi chemāh prajā iti.
Tvang hi sanghāra buddhyātha pradurbhūtā ruso mama,
Tasmāt sanghara sarbāngstvang prajāh sajarhapanditāh.
Mama tvang hi niyogena tatah shreyo hyabāpsyasi.

(Ibid. 20-22)

In spite of this clear assurance from her own creator Death took serious exception to this most unpleasant job. She prayed that she should be spared that sad duty. She gave her reason in greater detail. The crux of the plea is she was afraid of sin (Adharma), she would have to take away the dearest thing that ever man had, their life; it would be the most tragic experience to see them lose their nearest and dearest ones.

The Creator appreciates the sentiment thus expressed by Death, but she must know the other side of the truth. So he explains to her saying, 'Death, you have been intended for that (*Sankalpitasi*), for the destruction of life (*Prajasanhārhetuna*), it is an inviolable principle; hence you will commit no sin; nor will you be blamed for that'—

Bhabitā tvetadebang hi naitajjātvanyathā bhabet,
Bhaba tvaninditā loke kurusva bachanang mama.

(Ibid. Chap. 54, 11)

Even after Brahma's clear explanation of the nature of the whole truth, of which life and death form only two indispensable parts, Death was afraid to bear a hand. She begged him not to ask her to do it. What should he do now when Death pleads her fear of sin and her compassion for the victims ? He cannot surely advise one to act otherwise. He could not therefore take a peremptory attitude to her prayer, rather he kept calm, as if content within himself at the sentiments just expressed. Death, too, seemed to have been inwardly inspired by the moving silence of the Creator, and in her elevated mood tacitly passed time. It was love that filled his mind and there was complete absence of wrath :

Tūsnīmāsīt tadā debah prajānāmīshvareshvarah,
Prasādang chāgamat kshipramātmanaiba prajāpatih.

(Ibid. 13)

So Death had no fear of his wrath now, she passed in a mood of worship and adoration, and soon reached Dhenukasharma for self-purification through austere spiritual courses to be observed there undisturbed.

Death took a very difficult vow and abandoned all comforts of life : she was undergoing the most excruciating penance although she had committed no sin yet : she was doing it practically to propitiate her creator and avoid the already assigned painful task of killing. She thus passed thousands of years just like a secluded nun—we are to know in the Mahabharata it is an accepted convention to use time and space with the utmost flexibility, both ways in unlimited extent and the extremity of its concentration. The text has elaborated in so many words the inconceivable austerity with which she observed the vow over an unusual extent of time.

God is pleased when one is pure at heart or when one sincerely tries to be so. Brahma took kindly to Death's efforts at self-purification and asked why she were following that self-tormenting method of sanctification. She told him imploring, 'Father, I am afraid to take away their life who do cherish it in their own self grudging none their own. For fear of sin I then take this very difficult vow.'

Brahma gently persuaded Death and repeated his earlier plea only with further elaboration. He assured that in her act of destruction Yama (the ruler of the under world), the diseases and the gods would come to her help. It would drag her into no sin. Death bowed her head and humbly took the charge that was entrusted to her saying 'when it will not be done except by me I shall be doing it, but before I am to do it, Father, you must grant me one humble prayer, you must make the living body vulnerable for the access of avarice, anger, lust, envy, obsession and transgression, all these devious passions, to it.'

The Creator readily granted it—

Tathā bhabisyate Mrityo sadhu sanghara bhoh prajāh

(Ibid. 39.)

He granted it and ensured that all the tears she had shed for love and compassion into the hollow of his palm would turn to all the various diseases in living bodies endemic and self-infective—

Yānyashrubindūni kare mamāsangste byādhayah
prānināmātmajātāh

(Ibid. 40)

She has no cause to fear that she is doing it. All the living things must come to their end, and she will have to act as the divine agency of the Creator. Brahma then enjoined how she should do it and how she could benefit from her doing it.

Death must not do her part out of grudge or anger, or any desire for herself, she has no occasion for that, she is to do it only as an enjoined sacred duty, enjoined by her Creator and the Creator of everything else. This will save her from cruelty and sin, there can be no sin in what the Creator wants you to do, you fall rather from not doing it. The Creator gave her to understand that she would act as a mere tool of a higher order, Dharma—

the eternal principle—which will not brook those who violate its laws :

Mithyābrittān māryisyatyadnarmah

(Ibid. 42.)

By acting as an instrument of inevitability or necessity Death can very well make herself pure—

Tenātmānang pābayasvātmanā tvang

(Ibid. 43.)

This is how Death is persuaded to do her work. We know this is the story of Death narrated by Vyas Deva from a remote source traditionally accepted as authoritative. King Yudhisthira was thus consoled as in a still remote age was Akampana by Narada.

(3)

The birth of Death is a part of the evolution which started from the creation of life. In their order of precedence life came first then death as a counterbalancing stroke. Both together made an entire cycle. When first life came on earth the only problem surely was how to sustain the cause of life and fill the lonely planet with it. The Bible has acknowledged it in that providential decree 'Be fruitful and multiply.' The same problem must have been experienced at the dawn of life on this part of the world. The other problem of the explosion of population must have been felt much later. In that very ancient stage of human existence and evolution this problem was sought to be solved in a different method from the modern family planning. The Rishis of India—the self-appointed guardians of truth and principles—must have seen a solution in the very order of life itself. In their realization the truth of death must have flashed, they made it a part of a myth as they had done in regard to many revealed truths.

The story of death, the ultimate end of all life, symbolizes a sort of divine family planning. The whole world is the Creator's family which he has planned with both life and death, one set against the other. Death is no sin when it comes as a relief and not as a shock to life, the whole myth seems to convey this idea. Death when it comes as the natural end it causes no shock, neither to its natural victim nor to the world at large. People seek relief through death when life is no charm to them, rather an unbearable heavy burden and a sad task for others to help them along. There is nothing strange or unnatural in death.

When Narada or Veda Vyas was expounding the principle of this eternal truth they were not at fault, but when they applied it to that specific case they met they seem to have served a different purpose than truth. Neither of the deaths they sought to explain in a consolatory manner was natural death, they must have seen it, but consolation was their main issue, and with that end in view they adopted the right method, they unwrapped the secret of death itself. But the difference which they understood quite well is that here death is not a source of relief but a grievous shock. Abhimanyu and Hari both died fighting their enemies in their blooming adolescence. They died, but not without reason, death is not a causeless injury, the Mahabharata has not painted it as such. The Mahabharata myth, have not distorted truth, they have only dressed it up and made it more attractive. Death is normally a balancing force as against life and a part of necessity. There is nothing unpleasant in its normal course, but when death occurs before its normal time it shocks us, although it is not irrelevant or out of place. Abhimanyu's death is not painted in the Mahabharata as the blow of blind Fate, I have attempted that episode elsewhere as partly in this book next.

Death is painted here as a disinterested but not blind force, disinterested as the law of nature, but not blind as an undeserved injury. Death is given to act without any grudge or a desire of her own, the expression in the text in this connection is—

Kāmarosau sangtvajya tvang sangharasvehajībān

(Ibid. 42.)

It is also enjoined that created beings would die by their own choice against life tempted into the trap of dissipating excess of passions which bring in their train so many distempers of the body. According to the Mahabharata *mithyābrittān* are those who act against the principles of life called Dharma. So *mārayisy-atyadharmah*, Adharma—violation of the principles of life causes death. Shockingly enough death comes before its time, when it would have marked a normal end of a course of evolution like sunrise and sunset, and left no scar of tragic experience.

The myth of the unwilling Death reveals a significant side of the Indian view. Death is represented as love, for love of life she would not destroy anything. She shed tears which gave rise to various diseases, we know. The truth of this part of the story is, in the scheme of creation there is no death that does not help the cause of life, death which is against the nature of life is caused by unlove, by an apathetic attitude to life itself. People die before their time because they do not respond favourably to the love that death bore to all created beings. It is due to sheer unlove that people act against life; and death comes when they do so, and takes its birth in the inevitable reaction of such a choice.

The episode has another great truth to reveal. Death was inspired by a deep love for the creation which Brahma being the creator could not discourage, so he kept silence over it and gave her to follow her own sense of the right, we have seen. This course adopted by Death, however justified in itself, brushed aside a truth which attains its depth and significance only in relation to everything else, to the whole scheme of creation. What it is only the Creator is in a position to know, his will is the revelation of that secret; nothing incompatible with it, however apparently just in isolation, is really so. Death was first misled in her own pragmatic ideas and emotions. The Creator waited for things to settle down, for Death to see the illusion of her love, it was a love that ignored another love—the love for her Creator, which undoubtedly could open her eyes to the whole purpose of things. Brahma drew her attention at last to that cenrtal love which would give meaning to all her loves and without which those loves would surely prove a trap to her and lead her to the mirage of total meaninglessness. Brahma wanted her, as everything else in the Universe, to play her part in the whole order that his wish has only taken a concrete shape of. What appears to be out of place and irrelevant from a partial view as of Death here, is quite in place and well-linked in the whole view that is his who has everything well-comprehended within himself and given everything its due share in that order.

KRISHNA CONSOLES ARJUNA AND SUBHADRA

This chapter of the Mahabharata deals with the inevitability of death which is caused by the secret hand of destiny where even the Ordainer of all things can but stand as a helpless spectator. Krishna appears in that role with regard to the death of Abhimanyu. His role is unique in itself. The article explores all its bearings upon truth and realities.

(1)

Towards evening Arjuna was on his way to their own camp in the chariot under Krishna's conduct after the day's victory in war. But his mind was constantly haunted by misgivings and apprehensions of coming evil. He asked the reasons of all this unnecessary mistrust. Krishna assured him that they would ultimately win, and the loss on their side would be quite limited. It is to be noted that Krishna never assured them that they would remain absolutely unscathed in this war, especially in this case a retort of this kind has an exceptional import. Krishna, the Ordainer of all things, knew what could happen and when. Abhimanyu's death is really ordained by fate, the fate made possible by the invisible imperceptible reasons of his birth and an even remote reason of the parents' marriage. Fate in Indian conception is an effect upon a tangible physical plane from a far remote plane of causality beyond usual everyday perspective. It is invisible but inescapable. In his subdued tone of encouragement Lord Krishna did not rule out entirely a loss they would incur by reason of this kind of destiny.

How Subhadra and Arjuna deserved this destiny of Avimanyu's death requires a retrospective appraisal of their conjugal relationship and affinity, which is done in the next article. Lord Krishna as Lord has always to advise life, even in the highest impediments to it, as much as it yet be left secure. Abhimanyu's untimely death cannot be averted, so he had better prepare Arjun's mind for that inevitability. Arjuna sensed aright,

Abhimanyu did not appear to accost his father upon his return from the battlefield, because he may have lost his life in his absence in that tricky battle of mazy array of troops in the form of a wheel called Chakrabyuha ! He repented that he taught him only how to break into this special arrangement of troops and did not enlighten him as to how to break out of it :

Nāchopadistastasyāsīnmayānīkād binirgamah

(Drona Parba, Chap. 72, 21)

It is strange to note that Krishna had already heard Yuyutsu proclaim a warning to the embattled army of the Kauravas that they encircled the boy hero unlawfully in the absence of his father. Arjuna accused Krishna why he did not report it to him in time. Krishna did not, possiblly because it was inevitable. So he only consoled him, quoting stipulations of the leaders of religion. He told Arjuna, Kshatriya heroes are fated to die in battle, that is the highest attainment of their lives. Abhimanyu has attained this glory, Arjuna had better console his mourning brothers. Lord Krishna could turn Arjuna's mind to heroic glory and noble activity for retaliation of his son's death : but once more Arjuna moved in a way which required Lord Krishna's personal care and correction. Practically Krishna did it all through the Kurukshetra drama.

Arjuna's heroic spirit rose for retaliation, he vowed to kill the killer of his son next day certainly before sundown and pledged to destroy himself in the burning pyre if he failed. This led all the heroes on the Pandava side to think and induce Lord Krishna to think about its means. Arjuna pledged it without consulting Krishna, and did not think at all—it was quite impossible under such unusual excitement—what risk it involved. It is clear from Arjuna's vaunting even after Krishna's pointing to it that the hero was not well-versed in diplomacy and subtle army manoeuvre. He was confident of his strength, but did not take into consideration the countervailing move on the enemy side. He asked Krishna not to worry because he could not see what Krishna could in his unclouded vision. Arjuna left Krishna for the night repose requesting him to get the chariot ready just at dawn and in perfect battle order; moreover asked him to console the other inmates of the household, particularly Subhadra and Uttara, Abhimanyu's mother and wife respectively.

(2)

That night Krishna entered the closets of the ladies in Arjuna's household for a little solace that he could offer even when he would be thinking of the strategy of the next day's battle. Krishna's presence increased Subhadra's moan by contrast. Abhimanyu had Krishna for uncle and Arjuna for father, particularly Krishna who is known to be the Lord of the Universe. Subhadra referred to this contrast in her lamentations. But Krishna was helpless, he could not save Abhimanyu in spite of his best wishes.

He comforted Subhadra in words that suggested how helpless he was in the work of destiny. He asked her not to lament with her daughter-in-law, for it was useless, this is the end of all living objects ordained by fate :

Sarbesāng prāninãng bhīru nisthaisā kālanirmitā

(Ibid. Chap. 77, 12)

In this drooping state of their minds at the loss of their dear son Krishna cannot refer to their marriage, to the circumstances in which it took place. He only referred to fate. It is part of fate that Arjuna omitted to teach his son the tricks of exit from that special formation of troops. Abhimanyu died a heroic death, the death destined for a Kshatriya, Krishna told his sister.

Subhadra, in her lamentations, recounted how happy a life her son lived in the palace and wondered what a change it meant to see his body besmeared with blood and dust and left unattended. Not all her account was that of a well-principled pious life. Abhimanyu must have inherited the flighty and ill-principled nature of his parents both before and during his procreation. In this connection Arjuna-Subhadra marriage is to be noted. The mother was lamenting the wretched death of her son, a complete change of lot. He was used to enjoying the whole night among court courtesans, yet he was now fated to pass night in the field among jackals ; thus the mother was moaning :

Yoanvāsyata purā bīro barastrībhirmahābhujah,
Kathamanvāsyata soadya shibābhih patito mride.
(Ibid. Chap. 78, 7)

What life the young sprig lived in the palace is even more clearly suggested by indirect references in her invocation to meritorious life hereafter for her son. When she knew better the irresistible destiny her son had met she wished him the merits of all sacred lives none of which was practically his in his sportive exploits hithertofore. It would be a long story to narrate all these. Only some significant passages are pointed out here. The moaning mother wished her son the end which could be the saints' earned by years of Brahmacharya (continent life of the highest good) and the end of the life of undeviated single love. She also wished for her son the goal of the high-souled who cleave only to their wives and be physically engaged to their consorts in times of menstruation quite averse to another's spouse :

Ritukāle svakāng bhāryāng gachchhatāng yā manīsinām,
Parastrībhyo nibrittānāng tāng gating braja putraka.
(Ibid. 32)

Subhadra wished her son to attain that state of bliss after death which God-fearing people may attain by their meritorious acts. Some of them which are noted above, and noted *inter alia*, are supposed to have never been practised in Abhimanyu's own life. He was a Kshatriya youth, essentially of a heroic spirit and given to all the pleasures of life, naturally not all within the scope of continence. The demoniac strength of his body and the courage of his mind were not well-balanced with the control of the spirit. Krishna knew it and knew why, and knew no less where it may end.

Even a dear love, if it is at all so, cannot be held outside a necessitarian purpose. Lord Krishna took Kurukshetra war for an inevitable necessity. It drew many a life to a close, ordained by their respective fate. Abhimanyu is a case in point. However great the loss, Lord Krishna did not mourn it unless for temporary consolation of those severely affected. It is his godly nature to share every woe although he knew its reason and could not avert it by a careful adjustment at source long before. Now Krishna mourned for the mother when he saw her faint. His reason for mourning is quite different. He must have thought things could have been otherwise, knowing this made him all the more helpless than even the actual sufferer. Subhadra fainted, and he wetted her with water to revive sense and nursed her as sincerely as he could. He asked Droupadi to give constant company to Uttara in her mourning.

Lord Krishna cannot but suffer with the sufferer, but he is never to be lost in it but for a moment, his circumspection is all too expanded for that ; he does naturally connect everything to a totality of origin and effect. So he left the ladies' boudoir for Arjuna's apartment where he arranged the night's rites for the hero who would pass through a very difficult feat next morning. He had Arjun's bed made, lending a hand in it too, with all the god-inspiring materials scattered upon it and all heroically inspiring weapons all around it. Then after a short but sweet exchange of civilities with the hero Krishna left the place for the night.

How Arjuna spent that night is quite immaterial here. He worshipped his ideal god Mahadeva, or finished the rites with the help of attendants. Quite natural his physical response and repose would be absolutely disturbed by the impatience to meet the enemy next morning. But how did Krishna pass the night ? It is quite significant. He went to bed but enjoyed no sleep at all. Going to sleep was absolutely impossible. He knew Arjuna had vowed a very difficult vow, to kill the killer of his son before sundown or to destroy himself in the fire. Krishna knew there was many a mischievous trick which they might play to defeat it. He was then calculating in his mind the next day's war strategy, how to frustrate all their stratagems and evasions, and how to fulfil Arjun's vow and avert a greater risk. In his anxiety to make the next day's victory doubly sure Lord Krishna began to talk to his favourite car master Daruka who must have been by his side that night to hear what he may have been ordered to make any special arrangement. Krishna thought of any possible way to save Arjuna, he espoused his cause as his own so much so that he began to conceive the idea or Arjuna's being half his own existence, just his alter ego. He told Daruka in the same vein, as he told him his anxiety about it. Daruka was asked to place all the best weapons upon the chariot and to get ready the best of the chariots to meet any eventuality. He knew that Jayadratha whom Arjuna vowed to kill would be protected by the best of war heroes and the war master Dronacharya himself. It would be a very difficult feat and he must meet it.

Lord Krishna prepared the warrior who would inevitably be his instrument. He started it from the night when he made his bed with his own hand, the text conveys this idea :

Tatoarjunasya bhabanang prabishyāpratimang bibhuh,
Spristvāmbhah Pundarīkākshah sthandile shubhalakshane.
Sangtastāra shubhāng shayyāng darbhaibaidūryasangnibhaih.

(Ibid. 79, 1-2)

He made the bed with all the sacred things like Kusha grass as white as that special kind of gem called Baidurya and upon a sacred ground bestrewn with fired rice and flowers and some of the sweet-scenting balms. He wanted to inspire an elevated mood in the hero and make such an impression of his personal touch upon all that Arjuna even in his sleep could feel his divine presence. Krishna knew the next day's victory would require most the providential intervention, whether Arjuna knew it or not. Lord Krishna was that providential incarnation, and his touch in Arjuna's life would supply him with the strength and spirit in this drooping lamentation. Krishna's making the bed for Arjuna was surely an especial kind of grace through which Arjuna could sustain his sinking nerves by his personal touch with the Lord in dream. The deep impression of Lord Krishna's care in his bereavement resulted surely in the direct vision of Krishna.

Arjuna dropped off to sleep in his mourning that night while repeating the sacred Name which he got through initiation. In his sleep he had a vision of Lord Krishna appearing to him while he lay extremely distressed by the loss :

Tang tu shokena sangtaptang svapne kapibaradhvajam
Āsasād mahātejā dhyāntang Garurh dhvajah.

(Ibid. Chap. 80, 2)

Krishna's appearance in his dream turned the scale towards complete relief and a great sense of assurance. Then started an incomparable experience with Krishna by his side although in vision. In dream Arjuna rose from his seat as he always did at the sight of Krishna. Krishna too gave him timely counsel for the next day's battle. It was Arjuna's mind in repose that went thoroughly behind the impediments in his way to realize his vow, which took the shape of a dream associating itself with the highest resort of his life, Lord Krishna. In the excited state of his mind Arjuna thought only of killing the enemy but never of the means nor of the obstacles in the way. Now in the composed state of his mind particularly attained under Krishna's tendance he could thoroughly examine the problem although in dream. The occasion was practically created by Krishna's soothing touch.

Krishna asked Arjuna in that dreamy state to shake off all grief and think of the means of success in the next day's battle. This must have been a turning-point in Arjuna's mind, which showed a clear awareness of the possible difficulties he was to face. He disclosed all these in his dream to Lord Krishna. He did not brag now as he did earlier, he detailed all the impediments in the way, even the great valour of Jayadratha his enemy and the short span of the day due to the sun's motion in the southern hemisphere. He asked at last the means of fulfilling his pledge to save his life. It is a clear case of submission to Lord Krishna's counsel, though of course in dream. The submission itself gave him solution. Solution remains in one's own self only benighted or mute under severe personal obsession. Submission to a higher ideal, the highest in the scale the omniscient Lord of creation, removes it and causes self-awakening and clear insight. Arjuna must have attained it during his dream. The means of victory flashed upon his mind, which in proper mythical form, psychological too, came from his contact with Krishna in dream. Krishna asked him to invoke the weapon called Pasupat once Lord Siva's possession. Arjuna could not at once call it up. So Lord Krishna advised him to mind that Lord and meditate.

Upon Krishna's instruction Arjuna started the rite and in the midst of it was transported to a higher region with Krishna clutching his right arm. They rose higher in the air and passed through beauty spots of that mountainous region where Lord Siva held his seat. Flying through the whole region they at last reached the place where they saw Siva seated in a posture of highly concentrated meditation. Both Krishna and Arjuna bowed their head before him, and at once there was established a spiritual channel of communication between them. Lord Siva could know the exigency of the circumstances which drove them to him and assured them of his full support. Then Arjuna prayed for a boon of divine weapons. Lord Siva immediately granted the prayer and pointed to a nectarine Lake not long way off from his seat. He would find there that weapon, the missile and its launching instrument, which Lord Siva used long ago against the demons. But when Krishna and Arjuna reached the lake they found no such weapon but only two giant snakes. To their great surprise the two snakes gave up their snake form and assumed the form of a giant bow instrument and its arrow missile. They took them to Lord Siva and from one side of the Lord was born a penance-sanctified hero to demonstrate the use of it to Arjuna. Arjuna observed with utmost care the position and posture of the divine demonstrator to be well-taught in the art. Then Lord Mahadeva gave him the weapon called Pasupat and pronounced the boon, 'Be released from your vow.'

The means of victory is got and the dream ended. Through Lord Krishna's care and contact the dream restored not only his tranquillity of mind but at the same time made a careful consideration of his battle strategy possible. All these happened to Arjuna the while Lord Krishna passed his night talking to Daruka, his car master. He too could not enjoy a wink of sleep that night. The day then dawned and all the preparations of war began. Yudhisthira woke up early to attend to all the rites of daybreak. There was a visible stir in all quarters yet with self-enjoined silene everywhere.

(3)

At dawn when Yudhisthira already finished his morning prayer streams of war heroes of his army sought his audience at the gate of the outer apartment. They were all shown in. Then came Lord Krishna for the morning visit to the eldest Pandava. They first exchanged civilities and asked after their mutual well-being. All these done in perfect court etiquette Yudhisthira came to the question of the day's war-stake and in presence of the Kshatriya warriors he implored Lord Krishna for his unfailing help in it. Yudhisthira completely surrendered to Lord Krishna as the best resort. He said, "Lord, thou art our only help, only support as the Indra to the gods, we want to attain victory and happiness only through you. You know all our stakes in life, know also about the dangerous vow of Arjuna, I pray my mind be always set upon you, and Arjuna's pledge be fulfilled through your grace . . . " He made a long prayer to the Almighty Lord, he took him for that in their great danger. In their single-minded surrender Krishna saw the best opportunity to serve them and their cause, the Lord is apt to do it only through undeviated concentration of mind of the suppliant which establishes communion with him and the resultant inward awakening.

Lord Krishna assured Yudhisthira all help, and narrated how Arjuna, best of the heroes, would be quite competent to meet the situation in the battlefield and he would personally supervise all to victory. He told Yudhisthira that Jayadratha would surely not escape death even if he be protected by Indra and his divine cohort, and told him that Arjuna would do everything for the final victory. King Yudhisthira would, of course, depend entirely on the Lord, the highest source of divine help.

Krishna knew what he should do. Arjuna came just at that time to both the king and Lord Krishna. He looked gleaming with a lustre all over, which Yudhisthira remarked at the first sight. He narrated how by the grace of Lord Krishna he saw Lord Siva in a strange vision. Arjuna was then quite a different man, although he did not fully know how everything was carefully arranged to that effect by Krishna. He was now confident of victory as all the courtiers and heroes were, seeing that remarkable change even in his person. They all then withdrew, the time for battle was near, Lord Krishna attached so much importance to the day's battle that he decorated the best of chariots with his own hand, endowing it with all the auspicious signs of divine inspiration:

Tatra gatva Hrisīkeshah kalpayāmāsa sūtabat,
Rathang rathabarasyajou bānararsabhalakshanam.

(Ibid., Chap. 84, 11)

Once Krishna made Arjuna's bed, we know why. This time too he took personal interest in the decoration of the war-car which Arjuna was to use. He made all the plan of decoration, lent a hand to it to ensure extra grace so that the war may be inspired by a sense of divine responsibility. When the car was in complete battle array Krishna personally came to report to Arjuna his preparedness. Already divinely inspired by the night's dream and in constant touch with Lord Krishna thereof Arjuna got ready to ride the car and did not forget to walk round it repeating the abracadabra of war and signs of victory. They both rode upon it as if shining like the twin Aswinis seated side by side. Their very existence there enforced a favourable reaction in nature. There blew wind redolent of sweet smell and with sounds and serenity of atmosphere nature signified coming victory in war.

The Kaurava army knew that the day would be a dismal experience for them, Arjuna would be more terrible in his fight for retaliation than usual. Dhritarastra, the blind king, sensed all the portents of total massacre that morning, no encouraging sounds in any corner of their camp were heard, particularly Jayadratha's camp remained silent as dead. The blind king recounsed all their past mistakes to the clear-eyed Sanjaya and Duryadhana's misdeeds. He mourned to him that victory is certain to them whom Lord Krishna guided even by reining the horse for them and Arjuna represented as the mailed first :

Tesāmabhīsuhastah syādbisvakseno rathe sthitah.
Sangnaddhashcharjuno yoddhā tesāng nāsti parājayah.

(Ibid. Chap. 85, 44-45)

He then wanted to know their army's strategy to face the exigency. The king was visibly worried. Sanjaya reprimanded the indulgent king to stolid indifference at this stage of no return and assured him of an accurate description of their preparation. He gave a long account of the field. We must not go into those almost endless details, but we must narrate how ultimately by Krishna's war strategy Arjuna fulfilled his vow. Dronacharya, the great master of the science of war, disposed troops into a special battle array like a needle-penetrating concave and placed

Jayadratha in that impenetrable point to baffle even the closest possible search for him. The front and different other stages of attack were strongly guarded by different companies of troops under different local commands of proved efficiency. Krishna knew the search would be very difficult unless it was made easy by other tricks. Towards the close of the day Krishna thought of one such war trick. He created an illusion of darkness to lead the enemies to think that the day had ended. He must have influenced natural phenomenon by some scientific process of Yoga for only a temporary effect. This trick he played quite successfully. Jayadratha came out from his secure hiding place in joy, but only to meet Arjuna and his own end.

Krishna would not resist what is inevitable in the course of nature. He could not resist Abhimanyu's death, it was his mother who measured up the child's entire prospect at birth, even longevity, by her especial kind of association with her husband and an ill-assorted match which was interdicted by an uneugenic blood relationship (a different article is written on this head). Krishna did all in his power to avert this marriage, but when this marriage took place it must take its natural course. Lord Krishna stood apart from the whole issue, rather a helpless spectator and did only that which he could to console the parents and to guide the strategy of war for a proper retaliation. There Krishna did not obstruct the course of nature, but only created an illusion by some scientific means perhaps, deepest of the kind in Indian spiritual realization.

SUBHADRA ELOPED

People know only the apparent truism about Arjuna's elopement with Subhadra to which Lord Krishna lent his support. According to the contemporary social custom this marriage was wrong, although it was not yet so unequivocally pronounced as in the present Hindu laws. How could the Lord, being the manifestation in his own self of the still undetected truth of human life, support this marriage, a marriage within uneugenic blood-relationship ? The present article examines how far the Lord has done it and in what significant way.

(1)

Lord Krishna came to play his divine tricks in a human way quite within all human limitations as his incarnation as such has imposed upon his movements. He has made it clear to Saint Utanka in another Chapter of the Mahabharata :

Dharmasya setung badhnāmi chalite chalite yuge
Tāstā yonīh prabishyāhang prajānāng hitakāmyayā.
Yādā tvahang debayonau bartāmi Bhrigunandana,
Tadāhang debabat sarbamācharāmi na sanshayah.

* * * * * *

Mānuse bartamāne tu ... ...

(Asvamedhika Parba, Chap. 54, 16-20)

'I form the bridge of Dharma all through the ages while passing through them and in my wish to ensure welfare of the created things I get into my mother's womb. When I am born of a divine mother I behave like a divine, when in human form . . . I behave like a human . . .'

Lord Krishna did not change this nature when dealing with the Arjuna-Subhadra sensitive episode as in everything else. In the contemporary age marriage still remained an intractable institution in society, yet not entirely free from Primitive irregularities in man and woman relations, but at the door-step of Brahminic care and caution particularly under the realised leadership of the Rishis. The Kshatriya community made an especial case because of a large number of deaths in war among the young male section of it. The realised truth of Lord Krishna's life could not all be pronounced with the same accent particularly about marriage, in the midst of still prevalent irregularities. Of course very close blood-relationship, particularly within the same stock, had already been avoided in marriage or other physical contacts. Arjuna discarded the appeal of physical union from the side of Urbasi who, he tells us, belonged to the same line with him, and Urbasi on her side related in her reply a still earlier social convention now considered out of date. Let me quote those two indispensable passages one after another :

Iyang Pourabangshasya jananī muditeti ha,
Tvāmahang dristabāngstata, bijnāyotphullalochanah.
Na māmarhasi kalyāni anyathā dhyātumapsarah,
Gurorgurutarā me tvang mama tva bangshabardhinī.

(Bana Parba, Chap. 46, 40-41)

Anābritāshcha sarbāh sma debarājābhinandana,
Gurusthāne na māng bīra niyoktung tvamihārhasi.
Purobangshe hi ye putrā naptāro bā tvihāgatāh,
Tapasā ramantyasmānna cha tesāng byātikramah.

(Ibid., 42-43.)

A word for word translation of those passages would cover much space, let us have only the essence here. Arjuna explained to Urbasi why he was closely scanning her form. She was the Matriarch of the line of Puru in which he too was born. So she should not take it otherwise, particularly as an encouragement to physical contact which must be considered against all healthy principles. To this Urbasi took serious exception and referred to her never before meeting any such repulsion from the side of the scions of Puru. They were never averse to dalliance with her in their heavenly bliss. She renewed her appeal but Arjuna politely rejected it.

Arjuna's rejection of this ardent offer from the side of one of his own blood quite marks a stage in the evolution of eugenic sense through a casual reflection in an individual case. This same Arjuna broke laws in other cases, perhaps his ethical sense as noted above developed directly under the virtual discipleship of Lord Krishna had not matured yet for lack of spiritual surrender to the Lord's guidance from his side or an unconscious orientation of passion to that end. His intimacy with Lord Krishna was yet merely friendly, it did not deepen into a spiritual link, Krishna was not yet accepted by him as the incarnation of God.

Arjuna now left the capital for twelve years of pilgrimage, the occasion was caused by a breach of contract or the ethical principle involved therein. The five brothers agreed among themselves to share Droupadi whom Arjuna won by his valour and may have had the secret desire to get exclusively to himself. They accepted a convenient code of conduct to meet her one brother alone at a time, any breach thereof had to be expiated by a course of twelve years' pilgrimage throughout the country. Arjuna committed that breach, and committed under some psychological inducement no doubt. While he was roaming about the whole of India with a repulsed attraction for the lady he won for himself, he fell into bewitchment of women at different places. He fell prey to the charm of Ulupi, the daughter of the king of the snake region. But he made a curious compromise with his vow of incontinence (called Brahmacharya) in his approach to the princess. He asked her to think out a way as to how he could observe his vow as also fulfil her desire for physical union. Ulupi gave a psychological twist to Arjuna's affairs with Draupadi and ultimately got him for a single night at the palace to gratify her desire. With Chitrangada, the daughter of the king of Manipur, he had shown no such reservation and passed days there seeking gratification of his yet unsatisfied desire.

In such a frame of mind and bodily need Arjuna reached one of the holy places of India called Pravash, a place at a short distance from Lord Krishna's capital, practically it was their paternal seat of worship. There he met Krishna, of course the meeting was not due to his own initiative, rather it was Krishna himself who came to Pravash to meet his friend. The initiative from the side of Lord Krishna is significant. Arjuna had yet been roaming the places of pilgrimage of India, but had already been very lax in the austerity of incontinence by mixing several times with beautiful princesses. So Krishna may have indirectly pointed to this inconsistency of their covenant when he asked why he was visiting the holy places in that manner :

Kimarthang Pāndabaitāni tīrthānyanucharasyuta

(Ibid. Chap. 217, 3)

Surely Arjuna already in some sort of obsession could not sense the true implication of this covert broadside. Only visiting beauty spots or sacred places would not repair the wrong he has done, Brahmacharya (incontinence) is most needed for expiation, which Arjuna has failed to observe and failing which made all his pilgrimages nothing but pleasure trips. He explained to Krishna the cause of his visits but neither sought his help nor his advice. He could not yet consider him to be the sole source of Dharma. In social status and fame he was rather in a better position; when he passed through the thoroughfares accompanied by Krishna to reach their capital Dvaraka even ladies crowded at their doors and windows and roof corners for a convenient sight of the hero. Arjuna had a full consciousness of his importance and talked with Krishna at the Raibatak hill station a great part of the night about all the pleasant things of his long travel, practically everything but Dharma. He chattered with him as a friend, and not at all as a devotee or disciple. He talked about the beauties of lakes and rivers, hills and forests, springs and valleys that he had seen in those holy places :

Tīrthānāng palvalānāng cha parbatānāng cha darshanam,
Āpagānāng banānāng cha kathayamāsa sātvate.

(Ibid. 12)

(2)

All his travels marked no psychological recovery in him when Krishna met him. During his stay at Raibataka there was going on the annual festival of the royal family there. Originally it must have been a religious festival, but the royal family eventually brought about a different tone in the observance. Even the then ruler of the Brishni clan, Ugra Sen, was heavily drunk like a commoner. The whole city poured out into Raibatak hill and gave themselves up to passion and pleasantries. The hill resort turned to a complete scene of pleasure rather than a place of worship, with the court ladies dancing and singing, and the princes and courtiers of the palace recreating themselves in music and drink. Even the son of Rukmini and Samba, both born to Krishna, lapsed into noisy wassail. In such revelries only Krishna remained cool and composed taking the honoured guest round the whole scene. At one stage of this leisurely stroll Arjuna saw the maddening beauty of Subhadra who too dressed herself excitably in all sorts of garments and ornaments and was moving like a sportive deer. The very sight of her roused Arjuna's passion :

Dristvaiba tāmarjunasya kandarpah samajāyata

(Ibid., Chap. 218, 15)

In the light of the whole story of Arjuna's life of unfulfilled desire this will appear quite natural. Lord Krishna knew it and knew also that once Arjuna's passion was roused it could not be contained particularly in absence of an even stronger and higher absorption in his life. So he avoided direct exhortation and only left indirect suggestion partly humorous and partly persuasive :

Abrabīt purusabyāghrah prahasanniba bhārata,
Banecharasya kimidang kāmenalodyate manah.
Mamaisa bhaginī Pārtha Sāranasya sahodarā,
Subhadrā nāma bhadrang te piturme dayitā sutā.

(Ibid., 26-27)

'Why should the mind of a man in renunciation be disturbed by passion ?' Lord Krishna told Arjuna half humouring, and then introduced the maiden as his sister, by the same mother with Saran, of the name Subhadra and the beloved daughter of his father.

Krishna told him all these unasked only from a close scrutiny of some symptoms of attentions. His soft raillery and pointed description of relationship of the maiden in question are a modest persuasion to a restrained consideration of their relation that stood in the way of their marriage. Krishna knew a direct request would fall flat upon his ears. He took rather another indirect method, he offered to communicate Arjuna's interest in her, if he at all had any, to his father, curiously yet unasked.

In his passion-ridden state of mind it is hardly expected of Arjuna to take this hint. He took it just into the line of his passion and read just the opposite meaning in it. He told Krishna that Subhadra would be all the more acceptable to him for her being his sister and Basudeva's daughter, and asked him only to think out the means of obtaining her, if that be not absolutely beyond human power. Arjuna did not seek Krishna's advice regarding the ethics of marriage, which the latter would not waste offering unasked for. He knew direct opposition to Arjuna's wishes at this stage would come to no effect, rather complicate the issue. So he related the current custom of Kshatriya marriage, in this regard with some precautionary measure he could yet adopt. He sent out emissary to king Yudhisthira at Indraprastha and suggested the sure way of winning Subhadra to Arjuna when he pressed it hard, to forcibly take her away from Svayambara (self-selecting assembly of grooms), which was also according to the Kshatriya law of marriage. Krishna may have thought that Yudhisthira would give proper thought to its ethical side when it was against the law of Brahmacharya (incontinence), against their covenant and against social custom, eugenic impediment they did not know yet; and that the time-lapse up to Svayambara may cool down his passion. Arjuna's waiting for Basudeva's consent would also allow him time to think twice particularly on that old man's pointing to the wrong basis of such a marriage. Krishna may have thought about it too when he initially offered to convey it to his father for Arjuna. Arjuna did not take the hint seriously, his passion was too strong for that. So Krishna took the other restraining method, *i.e.*, waiting for Svayambra. But Arjuna could not wait even for that ceremony when a large number of Kshatriya princes would assemble to fight Arjuna in this attempt to carry off the bride. None of the restraining tricks worked. Subhadra was carried off from Raibataka hill.

(3)

Arjuna carried Subhadra forcibly and the heroes of the Yadava family took it hard and would chase him for reprisal. Again Krishna came to act his role to avert a great crisis which would come to no good on any side. In the family conclave they all blamed Krishna in one voice for the misfortune, even Balaram the sanest among the leaders brought the charge of secret complicity against Krishna. Krishna, however, did not divulge his secret motive and silent role to them, but only said and did things to avert a greater danger. He knew Subhadra's recovery was impossible and useless at this stage, she had already been taken away. Armed confiict would complicate the issue beyond reparation. He talked to the members of his family in a completely different tone, as if he knew well how thoroughly Arjuna considered the pros and cons of the issue. He told them plainly that Arjuna had done no wrong. He was a Kshatriya hero, so he did not think it glorious to win Subhadra in the groom-selecting ceremony, he preferred to win her heroically, which would increase the bride's honour rather than tarnish it. He must have considered it ignominous to the bride's family to buy her up for money. He was the pride of his family and an invincible warrior in the whole world. No doubt he would fight them to their deplorable defeat if they sought any military reprisal against him. So Krishna advised them not to add to the scandal, rather asked them to make peace with Arjuna proclaiming all merits of the case to them.

Krishana's stand at this stage seems to be contradictory to his earlier indirect methods of persuasion. But it is an essential part of his divine nature. He cannot forsake the sinner, rather he tries to limit the scope of the already committed sin and prevents, at whatever cost he can, the further spread of it. It is a clear case of this kind.

Krishna did it. He was susceptible to this marriage. He controlled everything to a limited evil. Under his well-reasoned instruction the Yadava elite decided to change their strategy and accommodate the scandalous situation that arose from Subhadra's elopement. All the war lords and ministers of the palace came to welcome Arjuna and proposed to solemnize the marriage. Arjuna agreed and after marriage remained in the Yadava capital one full year. After that Subhdra and Arjuna travelled extensively and spent twelve years at a holy place called Puskara. When Arjuna at last reached the capital Indraprasta the whole lot of the Yadava leaders rushed there with dowries of every kind, even more than usually they would have done in a negotiated marriage. The items of bridal gifts exceeded the formidable list of other Kshatriya kings. Came with them Lord Krishna himself, especially a little more careful than others to do them honour, the bridegroom and his family. He remained there when all other bridesmen came back. He had some special reason to do it, reason of his own, which was quite consistent with his divine nature. During the period of his stay in the Pandava capital something ominous would occur which he cannot leave unattended for its remote adverse impact. It was the birth of Abhimanyu, out of a marriage which was eugenically incompatible for the mixture of blood from the mother's side (Basudeva was Arjuna's mother's brother). It was yet not detected and recognized as such by the society, but it was one of the truths that were revealed to Lord Krishna, the seer of the age.

The birth of the child, although a convivial treat to the rest of the family, was surely considered by Lord Krishna as a bane rather than a boon, of course silently in his mind. He must have considered it a great misfortune to his sister and Arjuna. So he could not leave them alone in this moment of crisis in their life. He remained there, participated in all their rejoicings perhaps, as all of them may have sought him to do, yet it seemed not quite usual for him to remain so long in a sister's family for that alone. In the Mahabharata the name of the child is found etymologically punctuated when it was given :

Subhadrā susube bīramabhimanyung nararsabham.
Abhishcha manyumāngshchaiba tatastamarimardanam,
Abhimanyumiti prāhurārjuning purusarsabham.

(Adiparba, Chap. 220, 66-67)

Who gave this name and with two parts of the name broken for a special meaning to convey is not known. Most probably it was given by Krishna who then stayed with them. On another occasion Lord Krishna gave Parikshit his name referring back to the etymology of the root to make it connotative. The same method is adopted here, the two constituents of the compound separately convey the meaning of 'fearlessness' and 'moody' as Macdonell has suggested harking back to the Vedic use of the word Manyu (mood, mind) The name is so significant that it must have been given by one who is endowed with the insight into the whole prospect of the future life. He was born fearless but with a mind not quite wary and consistent, rather whimsical and impulsive, which is borne out by his future act in that last fight of his life. He could follow how to break into the centre of that special array of troops, but did not care to know how to fight out of it : the mythical construction of the episode may have only concealed this truth for a still more prying scrutiny. When he went to fight he did not at all think of the risk involved in it; however hard-pressed he was by force of circumstances he would have at least taken extra step to minimize it. He did not, on the contrary was carried by the fury of war. He was completely overmastered by the spirit of destruction, and was hardly aware of his personal danger, a complete thoughtlessness that overruled him. It is perhaps the same thoughtlessness which guided Arjuna under obsession of passion when he eloped with Subhadra the child's mother.

Krishna could not avert this crisis. It was destined by a wilful choice. The child was measured up by an impulse which excluded perhaps all thoughts of life and considered only fulfilment of their passion, and least of all the eugenic incompatibility of their blood. Krishna knew what none other could know. He bestowed best of his affection, perhaps to an excess, upon the eugenically handicapped child. Outsiders did not know why so much of Krishna's affection was reserved for the child. There is rather an apparant contradiction in Krishna's behaviour. He remained at the capital during his birth and himself observed the funeral rites after his death, as if it was his personal loss which nothing less than a prolonged mouring could mend. Yet he was indifferent to his death. He knew that it was coming, even he heard Yuyutsu warn the army against the wrong involved in an unequal fight, but did not call Arjuna's attention to it in time in an effort to avert death. Arjuna accused him and he simply referred to fate like an ordinary man of the world. In his human birth, as he has already stipulated, he imposes some human limitations upon him, and he never scales them except in a rare subtlety of human realization.

SHACHI THE QUEEN OF HEAVEN

Indra the king of heaven fell from his high position for a sin he committed to secure it from a prospective claimant named Trisira, a Brahmin of immaculate virtue and unbroken faith. The gods were without a ruler over them. The present article investigates into the matter that took shape in that interregnum, particularly concerning the Queen Shachi in absence of her royal husband.

(1)

Indra killed Trisira to ensure his position as king of heaven for life. Trisira appeared as a freak of nature with three heads symbolically serving three different purposes, whose interpretation requires a separate article that comes next. Indra killed him unlawfully out of envy. For this sin he had to abandon his heavenly home leaving his royal consort alone. The throne of heaven remained unoccupied for some time, which was against the law of nature. Even heaven, according to the Indian conception of ethical principle, cannot go well without a central authority to guide and restrain wherever it is necessary to keep everything on the right path. In absence of Indra that authority was lacking and in that god world and in nature there occurred preposterous things. There was always a class of people who had no official status as the gods had but who of their own accord dedicated their whole life and energy to the principle of divine life, and attained great knowledge of the mystery of the Creation. They were called Rishis and they offered their service on their own to the welfare of both god and man. They in particular and some of the gods took this void as a portent of great evil. They took care to look for one who could fill the gap at least on a tentative basis. They approached king Nahus for that. That it was simply a stop-gap arrangement may be seen from what Nahus himself said when approached by gods and Rishis alike :

Durbaloahang na me shaktirbhabatāng paripālane
Balabānjāyate rājā balang shakrehi nityadā

(Udyog Parba, Chap. 11, 4)

I am weak, I have no power to rule you all, a king must have power, that power lies in the Indra. Being only a ruler of the world Nahus pleaded his inability thus to rule heaven and earth both. So the Rishis, gods and the elite assured him of their moral and spiritual support which, they thought, would make up for his shortcomings. They told him their fear of one another in absence of a ruler. Under persuasion, therefore, Nahus agreed to be consecrated on the throne of heaven, but was categorically asked to rule all by the stipulations of Dharma : *Dharmang puraskritya sadā sarbalokādhipo bhaba.*

By the all-out support of heaven and earth Nahus became king of both gods and men alike, as in Indian history Gopal once was in a chaotic state of human conflicts and group rivalries by the willing submission of all to his authority.

No doubt king Nahus initiated rule of law and there was hardly any deviation from the principles of Dharma. But he could not keep up that spirit long. Indra's is the highest administrative post and one who occupies that position is entitled so. It is no personal name, but a rank. It must have some executive paraphernalia, some imposing formalities or procedural etiquettes, and even some indispensable grandeur attached to the mode of living in the palace. A Rishi would not accommodate his life of spiritual realization to all these. A different temperament is necessary for the post. So they selected a Kshatriya king. But the stipulation was, the king, in spite of all such privileges and splendour of life, must always stick to Dharma. The privileges enjoyed by the Indra were not a personal matter, but formed part of the highest executive rank, and surely for the sake of a psychological bolster. The Rishis knew it and therefore cautioned the newly elected Indra not to deviate from the principle for any temptation of the privileges and prerogatives his status partook. King Nahus could not act upon that timely pronounced warning. Even the king himself initially knew that he was not the best choice, but only the second best. Some days after his coronation as the Indra, all his awareness was gone, he was deeply engrossed in his royal prerogatives and forgot the principles.

He was so long always on the path of virtue, but now that he had attained to that high unattainable position, the ruler of heaven, he easily lapsed into the pleasure of the flesh :

Sudurlabhang barang labdhā prāpya rājyang tribistape
Dharmātmā satatang bhūtva kāmātmā samapadyata

(Ibid., 10-11)

So he gave himself up to roaming from one charming place to another which heaven provided for the pleasure of its divine ruler, now in the gardens of the gods, now in the Nandan, now in Kailash and now in the Himalayas, now in the seas, now in the hills and valleys, and now in the lakes, always accompanied by all the Apsaras (the court beauty of heaven) and divine girls, spending time in games and sports with them. When he gave sign that he would lead a life of ease and idleness all the heavenly dancers and singers, a race by themselves called the Gandharvas, the Apsaras and the Visvabasus attended to his pleasure.

King Nahus thus passed his days in idle pleasure for some time, and then got to find a new source of enjoyment, which readily suggested itself in the prospect of consorting the deserted Queen Shachi. He expressed his desire to the entire assembly of attendants and courtiers, 'Why does not the queen of Indra attend me ? I am now the Indra, and the ruler of gods and men too.'

Indrasya mahisī debī kasmānmāng nopatisthati,
Ahamidroasmi debānāng lokānāng cha tatheshvarah

(Ibid., 18.)

Queen Shachi saw the threat to her honour and chastity. So she approached the right person, the preceptor of the gods, Brihaspati, for help; and reminded him of a boon which he had earlier granted purporting that she would live ever happy, chaste and single-minded in love and affection, and would never have to wear widow's weeds.

Brihaspati reassured her, saying she would soon meet her husband and Nahus could not harm her. Now when Nahus learnt that the preceptor of the gods had taken Shachi under his protection he flew into a rage. The gods and Rishis who saw him in such a volatile state entreated him to give up all anger which did not become a man of his status. They begged him to consider that Shachi was the wife of another man, whom he could not embrace for the sake of virtue; and that he was the monarch of all the gods, which required him to rule the region according to the edicts of Dharma. Nahus did not pay any heed to their noble entreaties, he was too obsessed by passion for that. So he cited some misdeeds of the previous Indra, of which the most despicable was his assault upon Ahalya's chastity in absence of her husband Rishi Gautam. He referred to this episode of the past, probably because it formed a close parallel to his desired aim. He complained that the gods then remained silent and never raised their voice against many such sins and crimes of Indra. So this time too they must not stand in his way, they should rather do well to bring Shachi to him. The gods and Rishis saw good advice would not do, Nahus was after the gratification of his wicked desire, and this would soon lead to his fall as Indra had fallen for his evil deeds. They then appeased Nahus by a quick shift in their attitude, they agreed to do whatever he desired and even bring the queen of Indra.

The gods at last accompanied by the Rishis reached the residence of Brihaspati, the spiritual guide of the gods, and told him their godless errand. Shachi too was acquainted with it. She feared she would be sent away to the palace of Nahus as he had desired, so she began to sob turning her imploring eyes to the preceptor, saying she had no desire to be espoused to Nahus. Brihaspati repeated his pledge of protection and asked the gods and Rishis who came to mediate between them to think out means of tolerable good for both himself and the ex-queen of heaven. The Rishis and gods and the elite of the earth were really acting against their wish to plead for Shachi's acceptance of Nahus's offer. They were rather compelled. So they left it entirely to the divine preceptor to devise method. That Brihaspati then did. He suggested a trick that Shachi should go to king Nahus and beg for some time to offer herself ceremonially as his queen consort. No one knows what time brings in its course : there might crop up many an impediment in the way of fulfilment of the king's desire, he hoped. He was sure they would get over the sore point by this means. The visiting gods and Rishis expressed their full satisfaction over the suggestion and the prospect of relief. They retired to their respective places first appealing to the queen Shachi to act upon the plan. They assured her that her honour would not be touched, Nahus would fall for his unjust desire and Indra be soon restored to his lost position.

Thus Shachi was persuaded to meet Nahus and say what she was asked by the whole divan of the secret assembly.

(2)

Queen Shachi approached king Nahus to request that she be granted a reasonable period of time to see whether Indra could anywhere be traced and to make sure that she should marry him. In his passionate apprehension the very glowing appearance of the queen before him suggested itself as a sign of hope and a symptom of her willing submission. Nahus thought he could very well sleep over that reasonably short period the search might take. He granted her prayer. This part of the story as it is arranged here is really a threadbare expose of mere facts. The text of the Mahabharata depicts all the romance of a tremulous suspense which such a meeting may have caused.

King Nahus got absolutely pleased at the seemingly innocent proposal of Queen Shachi and gently sent her away to reach the residence of Brihaspati, the divine priest.

The gods were roused to serious consideration of a search for Indra by the very humble petition of Queen Shachi there. They thought out the means and ultimately approached Visnu who must have known where he could be, quite convenienced to do it for his comprehension in his own being of all that has been anywhere in the Universe. The patronymic distinction came from that special power perhaps. The gods also claimed that Indra accomplished the very difficult task of killing Vritta by his imparted spirit, by his encouragement, no doubt; he must have noted how he lapsed into a stupor through the killing of a Brahmin (the reference is perhaps to the murder of Trishira) and shunned the notice of all in a secret hiding. The gods then prayed that he should suggest means to remove the curse of deadness upon his nerves.

Brahmabadhyābhibhūto bai shakrah suraganeshvarah.

(Ibid., Chap. 13, 11)

Indra killed Vritta by the added strength of Visnu himself, that was perhaps no wrong, though, of course, Vritta's birth in the line of a Rishi, Tvasta by name, was caused by a cruel murder of the Rishi's son, Trishira, and out of the revengeful spirit roused in the father. By killing the demon Vritta Indra did a king's duty, but by causing the death of Trishira in a most cruel and clandestine method he must have incurred a natural curse. The difference between Indra and Nahus is in this respect to be marked. He got Trishira killed for fear of losing his throne in heaven, but he was not a confirmed sinner; although Nahus had pointed out a black spot in his character, which proclaims only some weaknesses of the flesh in him, the role that he acted in the killing of Trisira reveals only a weakness not more grievous than that. He was not a hardened criminal, rather he had a soul of goodness in him, which timely spoke against the wrong he might have committed. What he had done to secure his position from a worthier possible candidate reminds us of the innumerable political murders in our history, but the act, although committed under a threat of insecurity, was cruel and mean so much so that it later brought a shocked sense of injustice, to which all his sense organs revolted with an awful result of even physical stupefaction. He left his royal seat and even his wife in remorse, and led a life of complete isolation and secrecy.

Visnu took note of the situaton the gods related to him for his help. He advised them to ask Indra to observe the rites of a special kind of sacrificial fire known as Asvamed Yajna, it would release him from the curse of the sin arising out of the killing of a Brahmin and restore him to the position of the Indra. It is to be noted in this connection that Visnu asked for a sacrifice which would be directed to his entire satisfaction, *Māmeba yajatāng shakrah pābayisyāmi bajrinam* (Ibid., 14).

The reason is not far to seek, Indra had undergone a crisis of conscience, which resulted in a sort of nervous breakdown, an easy extension from the psychic to the physical plane. Visnu is proverbially the presiding deity of responsiveness, holding within his own being the total responses of the whole Universe, and thus rendering his omnipresence possible. The very word Visnu has that etymological implication, being formed of the root Vish (All pervader—Monier). The urgent need is, therefore, to bring back the lost responsiveness in the body and mind of Indra. He can do it only by a process of psycho-physical treatment, the sacrificial offerings to the deity of total responses seem to be only a mythical symbol of that formula.

Visnu gave the clue to reviving Indra's sense of his personality, which was absolutely lost in self-denial so much so that he never thought of his wife's distress in his absence. Visnu also warned the gods that they should take care to avoid conflict for some time, because Nahus would soon perish for his misdeeds.

The gods saw a ray of hope in the good advice of Visnu and persuaded Indra to undergo the sacrificial rites, which in themselves symbolized a process of expiation and made him feel like sharing the sin with others in life and nature :

Bibhajya brahmahatyāng tu brikshesu cha nadisu cha,
Parbatesu prithibyāng cha strīsu chaiba Yudhisthira.

(Ibid., 19)

But it only partly removed the settled gloom upon his whole personality, he came to the consciousness that he was not the only person to commit the crime, others too in some way or other, were involved in the killing of a Brahmin. With this awakened half-truth in him Indra came to usurp the throne from Nahus, but his still faltering heart failed him at the sight of another taking his place, which perhaps revived in him the horror of his sin and the terrible result of his downfall.

Dhūtapāpnā cha Bāsaboabhabadātmabān.

(Ibid. 20)

Only temporarily he felt himself cleansed of his sin in his senses. At the sight of Nahus on the throne of heaven he lost all his strength already regained and immediately fled the place to hide himself once more no one knew where. Thus Queen Shachi, missed him again.

(3)

Queen Shachi was lamenting her lot. Although the gods found out her husband and could bring him to her, he relapsed into that infirmity of mind and left both her and his royal abode. So all hopes were gone, how could she preserve her honour from the impending threat to it ? She was recounting all her virtuous deeds in the past, which did not merit such a plight. She was groping for what help she could get from whichever corner and invoked one after another the powers, which, she thought, could lead her out of it, and lastly called up the divine messenger, Upasruti, to be shown the way where her husband could be.

As in most cases so also here the truth has been mixed up in the usual mythical apparatus of the epic. Upasruti was only mentally conjured up, who, for the intensity of Queen Shachi's eagerness, appeared in human form bedecked with the divine beauty of heaven. The queen was after the most earnest search of her husband and naturally explored every corner of external help and went even to the most inaccesible part of the world for him, which she could not otherwise think quite possible without the guidance of the divine messenger. Although accompanied by her usual attendants, she must have been, being a queen and still in the highest care of the celestial priest, Shachi was convinced in her mind that she was chaperoned by the all-knowing Upasruti, or else she could not do what she had done. In this sense perhaps she was led by the divine messenger and reached a place she could not even dream that she would be ever able to get near.

She met Indra in a most unexpected corner of the earth, traversing a wide area dotted with hills, valleys, forests and unknown waters. It was a vast tract of land in the sea, a place of natural beauty with rare plants and creepers. She found there a picturesque lake bemused with the cackle of ducks and cranes of angelic beauty and sparkling with the glow of countless golden lotuses here and there. She found him there extremely bedimmed and shrunken that she had also to assume the same reduced state of body to meet him, which is described in mythical metaphors that she aided by Upashruti entered into the thread of a stem of a lotus, just splitting it, to find him there in his quintessential entity :

Tang dristvā cha susūkshmena rūpenabasthitang prabhum
Sūkshmarupdharā debī babhūbopashruti shcha sā.

(Ibid., Chap. 14, 12)

Now that Shachi met Indra in his benumbed and begloomed self it remained before her to adopt a psychological methad to reawaken his lost valour and dissipated vigour. She did never make her own state appear a sharp contrast to his, she wore a gloomy countenance all the more crumpled up in sympathetic response to his distress, which could demonstrate as if she too had retained all but her mere existence. This natural transformation in her appearance really avoided another shock and prepared the ground for the next step. She then in a mood of adoration and in all humility began to declare one after another all his past glories and merits, just to cover up his sense of guilt and the oppressed state of despair, and also to kindle in him the sleeping sense of responsibility and self-respect. He had already forgotten his past, even his wife. Now when his attention was drawn to it he could remember it and recognise his queen, and so asked her how she could know that he was there and why she had got there too.

Queen Shachi then narrated how Nahus with the three worlds under his domination had grown oppressive and was filled with pride; how he had asked her to accept his offer of marriage; and how she begged his leave for reprieve. She implored Indra to get out of that thread of that stem of lotus and assert himself and his power and establish his rule by the destruction of the wicked Nahus.

Consciously or unconsciously the part now Shachi played bore fruit. Indra came to his senses and considered his position and the way of restitution. He saw that he and his wife were in a difficult situation, which could not be met with sheer physical prowess. At that time Nahus remained more powerful than himself with the initial support of the Rishis and gods, they sought him to be steady on the throne of heaven in that period of interregnum and all their good wishes symbolized in their sacrificial fires went to that end, he explained to his queen. So a tricky method would have to be thought out for a remedy. He then suggested one to his queen, exactly the one that could totally forfeit the moral support of the Rishis, which might still be left after all Nahus's misdeeds. He asked Shachi to set one very difficult precondition upon her accepting Nahus; she should meet him with a humble desire—she must introduce it in an indulgent manner so that the power-puffed king, blind with obsessive desire, may not see the consequence—that he must be carried in a car drawn by the Rishis to her before the union could be solemnized. Shachi did it on the advice of her husband who still preferred to hide himself.

Queen Shachi met Nahus alone as if to confide her secretly entertained desire to him. Nahus accosted her with a simpering face, just standing up at his seat, and uttered sweet words to win her heart. He made a humble petition to her saying, "Ask a boon and it is yours. Don't be ashamed, rather speak out your mind, I shall accomplish it sooner it is done". The queen then took heart to say, "Noble king, the respite you kindly allowed has come to an end, now it is time to accept your offer, but I have some long-cherished desire that I must trust you with. If you do me this favour I shall be the more close to you for that." She made it clear that he must do something which even Indra could not : Indra had carriages of all sorts, drawn by elephants and horses, and chariots; he would, therefore, have to arrange such a conveyance as had not been sighted by the Rudras, Demons and the Rakshasas, and by Lord Visnu. Then she fanned his pride by a sort of peroration of high praise of his powers, and put forth the wish at the end of it to make it appear all the more easy : "You can take away others' glory by the merest evidence of your very shred of immense valour. None can stand your presence : you should not imitate gods or demons either; so high-souled king, let it be granted that you be carried in a palanquin borne upon shoulders of the great Rishis."

Under extreme infatuation King Nahus could not see where it would lead to. He became perfectly glad and was convinced that it would really be an incomparable conveyance and an enjoyable junket. He told her, "It is not within the power of a man only less valiant to harness the great Rishis to his car; so I have also the evident desire for it." Then Nahus descanted at length upon his excellent virtues and unquestionable powers, in fact to strike awe and wonder into her. "I am engaged in absolute self-purification and ordainer of all the three changes in the cycle of time, the whole world rests upon me. My wrath can bring an end to the whole of the Universe etc . . . . So darling, I must do your wish and immediately; the different grades of Rishis like Saptarsis and Brahmarshis would surely carry me; just see my glory and prowess."

Thus Nahus ended. Blind with pride of power that lewd king, sending Shachi away, yoked the spiritually disciplined Rishis to his vehicle for the journey to be made. Meanwhile the queen approached the divine priest Brihaspati to say that only a small part of the time fixed was left for Nahus to claim her and he (Brihaspati) would soonest lead her to Indra. He assured her saying she would have no cause for fear from Nahus, his end was very near when he had made the Rishis his carrier, moreover he would arrange a sacrificial fire for his destruction.

Brihaspati knew the secret of how Nahus's end would come. He was the king of the gods by the support of the Rishis and gods alike, once this willing submission was withdrawn he would fall like a pack of cards. His scrificial rites were only symptomatic and partly for Shachi's reassurance. The truth is Nahus must fall by his own sinful acts and by forfeiting the good wishes of all. The rites observed by Brihaspati would usher in a new era bringing an end to the oppressive rule of Nahus and preparing the ground for restoration of the deposed Indra to the throne of heaven. Brihaspati being the spiritual guide of gods and goddesses took the lead, and sought to trace the fleeing Indra. He must have tapped all sources to find him out, and sent whomsoever he thought worthy of the job to seek him. This is perhaps symbolically conveyed through the myth of the holy fire of the sacrifice being sent abroad to reach the remotest corners of the earth and even the most impenetrable part of it prodded by the urgency of the situation. It is just in keeping with the very style of the great epic. The fire searched every corner of the globe on land, but left out the seas where, he pleaded, he would have no passage. The king of heaven could nowhere to be found on land. The urgency of the situation required the fire god to enter into the sea even, the Rishi urged him; and by his added power, added by the very tremulous intensity of his eagerness, the fire god made way even through the water to seek him out.

All Rishi Brihaspati's persuasions came to this and the god of fire left him on his mission to search into the water. He traversed that vast distance to find Indra at the very lake where Shachi found him in her earlier search and in the very same condition, shrunken to his diminutive entity in the thread of a lotus stem. Shocks and surprises had caused an almost irretrievable depletion of energy in him. To excite vital force and rouse valour in him the divine priest Brihaspati took even more effective a step than was earlier adopted by Queen Shachi. He led the whole entourage of gods, Rishis and Gandharvas to meet him in that state, and began to narrate all his past glories and feats of prowess :

Gatvā debarsigandharbaih sahitoatha Brihaspatih,
Puranaih karmābhirdebang tustāba balasūdanam.

(Ibid., Chap. XVI, 13)

As spokesman of the assembly Brihaspati began in inspired terms to recount how he killed the demons Bal, Namuchi and Sambar, how he defended the whole world from the wicked assaults of the demons and how by the power of Visnu he slew the mischievous giant Vritta. He then drew his attention to the whole conclave of gods and Rishis who had arrived to ask his help. He urged him to recover his former self and extirpate the enemies—the enemies of life and culture *Bibardhasva sarbānchhatrūn nisūdaya.*

Also proclaimed, "None was mightier than you, none can be even now, only shake off inertia, that self-killing torpor, and rise once more to regain rule of the three worlds" : *Pāhi sarbāng shcha lokāngshcha Mahendra balamāpunhi.*

What Shachi's feeble and lone voice could not, was at once accomplished by the chorus of eulogy and the pledged support of gods and Rishis. The same support had once given strength to the hesitative Nahus, and it brought the same effect upon the drooping manhood of Indra. He was emboldened by the solidarity of support. This truth is mythically rendered :

Ebang sangstũyamānshcha soabardhata shanaih shanaih.
Svang chaiba bapurāsthāya babhūba sa balānvitah

(Ibid., 28-29)

Gloried like this he rose little by little to resume at last that lost physical stature replete with the vigour just revived in it. Only inspired he got out of that morbid state of contrition and self-reproach. In the limelight of his glorious deeds in the past he could yet see a prospect of his future, and thus begged the holy priest of the gods to say what more he wished him to do for the good of them all as he had earlier slain the mightiest of demons Tvasta's son Vritta. Brihaspati seized this opportunity to narrate all their tribulations at the hand of Nahus during his rule of the empire of heaven. Indra then asked, "What amount of meritorious penance and deeds of valour has made Nahus deserve the divine kingdom ?" In fact Indra was in so deep a nervous stupor that he could hardly care who ruled in his absence, he did not even care who ruled in his stead and how.

Brihaspati narrated how after Indra had left the throne of heaven there arose the need of a king in his place to avoid anarchy and lawlessness among the gods and the people of the world, the lower region being overruled by the region above. They sought out the foremost of the world-rulers, King Nahus, who at first felt diffident to shoulder that high responsibility; but finding none better than he the Rishis, gods and the leaders of the earth jointly decided to remove all his fears by their unqualified support and goodwill, and finally placed him upon the throne. Nahus was thus steadied on the throne and invigorated by the constant prayers that the Rishis and gods sent up for his sake. That earth-born king with his position so secure and his power unquestioned had grown intolerably impertinent to seek now to have him carried by the holy priests of penance, the Rishis. The gods and Rishis were now afraid of him and had withdrawn their love, but could not openly revolt. In this state of hellish impertinence Indra had not seen him. He must act as their saviour by removing Nahus from that position.

The very moment Brihaspati was persuading Indra to rise, first giving an account of the deplorable situation in heaven and earth, other gods too rushed there to plead for a remedy even more strongly. Kuber, Yam, Barun and Som, all these ministers of the people's cause got there and felt happy to find Indra in an unharmed state. Indra asked them to help him in his campaign of dethronement of Nahus. They, too, were relieved of their positions in those dark days; so they encouraged Indra to usurp the throne from Nahus, restoring them thereby to their original assignments. Indra made it a common cause with them and proposed to fight it out jointly. Even before the desired victory, the functionaries of heaven had their duties and assignments well ahead distributed amongst themselves by the consent of the deposed ruler Indra; even the god of fire (Agni), when he claimed his part, was apportioned his share in the administration by him (Indra), mythically called Aindragnya in the great sacrificial fire, an assignment perhaps next to Indra.

(4)

In the conclave of gods and elders Indra was then thinking of means for the destruction of Nahus, it was really in the nature of a secret court, only less noisy and less gaudy than Milton's Pandemonium. When deliberations were thus going on, Agastya joined them with the news of Nahus's fall from heaven. They did not yet know how it came about. So out of curiosity the king of the gods asked the Rishi, well-composed and all the rites of hospitality done to him, the very story of his fall.

Rishi Agastya at this related how it happened. Nahus had his vehicle carried by the grades of Rishis called Debarshi and Brahmarshi, the foremost among all the grades who engaged in the search of the mystery of the Creation through constant cultivation of both physical and spiritual sides of the self, when the power-proud king was thus moving along borne by the best of the men of penance, he was asked a significant question by them, when they got extremely tired under the burden. It was a simple question, at least it appeared to be so,

Ya ime Brahmanā proktā mantrā bai prokshane gabām,
Ete pramāṇang Bharata utāho neti Bāsaba.

(Ibid., Chap. 17, 9-10)

They asked if the king had any faith in the ethical principles and the sound-formula (Mantra) for the washing of cows, prescribed by those rare sects who knew the secret of the Creation (Brahamā). The question, although apparently unrelated, was quite in place and to the purpose. Had the king any such faith in the time-honoured principles he could not do what he was doing then. The king was, however, a beastly sinner, and had no respect for the ancient law-givers and the laws of life they discovered for mankind. He said 'no'. The Rishis who were then carrying the king's palanquin were extremely annoyed at this haughty reply. They made the cryptic comments, "You are in the path of sin and don't believe in the true religion, but we accept as ideal what the ancient Rishis postulated long long ago."

This led to an altercation between the king and the Rishis, and the king was so provoked that he ultimately kicked him on the head, Rishi Agastya told the inquiring Indra. As he did it under the impulse of a moment he was subjected to a stunning shock, which made him lose all strength and energy and all his kingly splendour. When the heat of his passion was gone he felt absolutely nerveless and cold. Rishi Agastya, too, as the spokesman of the whole lot pronounced a curse, "Oh, sinful king, as you have shown disrespect to the realized truth that came out of the ancient Rishis, and thus incorporated sins into their immaculate postulates; as you have become blind with the pride of your heart and planted a kick on my head; and as you have been getting the realized Rishis of unfathomed merits to carry you round the four corners of the earth, you have already exhausted all your accumulated virtues and forfeited this seat of perpetual bliss (heaven), you will have no power from today and fall down to the earth to crawl there as a snake for an inconceivably long period of time in expiation of all your wicked deeds here."

Indra and the whole assembly of gods took this news in the great glee of their hearts. Then the best of the trippers of the three worlds flocked there to accost Indra with their good wishes and requested him to take the throne of heaven which just then fell secure from his enemy.

Indra had already expiated his sin by prolonged suffering and by the purification of soul through sincere remorse all the time. When he thus attained that earlier purity of heart and proved himself worthy of the rule of heaven he was led by Agni, Bayu, Yam, Kuber, Barun and Brihaspati—all these leading deities of men and gods—to the seat of authority. There was again a fresh coronation ceremony with the chanting of hymns under the aegis of the divine priest Brihaspati. All his usual court attendants just accosted him with all ceremonial formalities. Thus came the end of that divine anarchy, the rule of law was restored under a benevolent central authority, and all the miseries of Shachi's conjugal life were over.

The episode indicates what ancient India thought of a divine rule. India never conceived an absolute absence of a central authority even in heaven, the place of perpetual peace and happiness, and even with a whole cohort of highly responsible and thoroughly conscious citizens of gods and Rishis. The presence of a divine monarchy could forestall a sort of divine anarchy, anarchy in a very noble form, but as it is anarchy, although in a refined form, it goes all the same the very same way with its grossest manifestation, reaching ultimately the same destiny. But a despotic ill-principled ruler in that central position brings not only his own end but also the endless misery to the ruled at large. The politico-spiritual order of ancient India would always provide for a perfect balance between these two forces—the political and spiritual values held tight in the closest possible harmony.

THE INDRA-TRISIRA EPISODE

The episode is sought to be laboured for the fact whether Trisira was a freak of nature, as he appears, or nature herself, and also for the true colour of Indra's sin, which ended in his downfall and justifiably confirms the truth of the earlier article.

(1)

The Mahabharata narrates the story of Trisira's birth. He was born to serve a special purpose. Why among the gods Prajapati Tvasta took upon himself to give birth to a child like that, is not immediately known. The text of the Mahabharata has not given it in clear terms; perhaps the narrator of the story felt no need to go into greater details, he was only relating to Yudhisthira for his consolation how even Indra, the king of gods, had to suffer endless misery with his spouse, when like him he was thrown out of his throne. He started where he should. But that does not mean that a great Rishi Tvasta did it without any reason. We are to know he was a Prajapati, a patriarch among the spiritually enlightened Rishis, having the self-imposed responsibility for replenshing this earth of scarce population with human beings of worth, not all Rishis took that responsibility, so all of them were not termed Prajapati. Prajapati Tvasta must have foreseen the ruling Indra's moral depravity and deviation long before it was manifest in actual misdeeds. He must have thought to bring forth one who could shoulder the entire responsibility of the ruler of heaven in his unfortunate fall. Indra was, no doubt, steeped in corrupted acts and ideas, and Trisira only fell an unlucky victim to them as many others must have been behind the iron curtain of the palace.

However, Tvasta took upon himself the responsibility of preserving a unified rule of law against a possible threat. A Rishi, as in an earlier article it is remarked, would not, by temperament, go to hold that position, it required a different temperamental combination. Rishi Tvasta, therefore, wanted to have a child who would do what he himself could not. Trisira was that child born to rule both heaven and earth.

Only outwardly his appearance seems to be freakish production of nature. He had three heads instead of one, with three different virtues to embody.

Bedanekena soadhīte surāmekena chāpibat,
Ekena cha dishah sarbāh pibanniba nirīkshate.

(Udyog Parba, Chap. 9, 5)

With one head he chanted the verses of the Vedas, one drank wine, and one devoured the four quarters, as it were, with eyes. This seemed to symbolize a contradiction in itself, but keeping in mind the style of the epic and the tradition of kingship in ancient India (as noted in an earlier article) one need not think so. The king, wherever he might have held sole authority, either on a higher plane of culture or lower, must combine in his personality diverse elements of apparently contrasted nature. Here the image evidently combines three such elements—the purity of a Brahmin, the passion of a Kshatriya, and an imposing personality apt to strike awe. This conception of a king imbibing the qualities of purity, passion and personality, still remains valid when they establish a perfect concord.

The then reigning Indra must have disturbed the balance by his many secret intrigues common to palace squabbles and power politics. Rishi Tvasta knew how indispensable the coherence of these elements was in a personality worthy to replace a corrupted king of heaven. Trisira was born as such a rare specimen in the evolution of mankind. Indra became envious of his very existence. He did not think of his own correction nor did he care to mend his ways, but wanted to get rid of him by any means. Trisira, however, had no envy, nor took caution to protect himself, he led his life as he was prodded by his inborn instict. He engaged in austere penance for self-purification, and to attain the state of equilibrium in mind and feeling. Indra was filled with envy at the austerity of his self-discipline and the vow of truth much too difficult for any man to observe. He did not, of course, think of killing him at once, but wanted to cause his moral degradation by some subtle indirect means, and thus to undermine his claim to the throne of heaven. He took it in his head to tempt him to the pleasures of the flesh, distracting his mind from the sole concentrated attainment of spiritual realization.

So thinking Indra called the Apsaras, the court ladies of heaven, to his assistance and asked them to put on their best attire and poise their limbs and carriage in the fullest thrill of passion, and to play all the tricks of love and throw all the glamour of rapturous beauty to seduce the mind of Tvasta's son in its highest trim of spiritual concentration. He thus enjoined the court courtesans of heaven to entice Trisira from the path of God into passion and pleasure. He told them of his obsessive fear. So he asked them to remove all his great fear and relieve him of his gnawing anxiety :

Asvasthang hyātmanātmānang lakshayami barānganāh.
Bhayang tanme mahāghorang kshiprang nāshayatābalāh

(Ibid., 12)

The palace courtesans did not know the strength of self-discipline Trisira was well absorbed in for communion with the Supreme Being. So they assured Indra of their readiness to approach that ascetic and cast the spell of bewitchment of their physical beauty and all their accustomed skill to tempt him into a life of pleasure. And this they actually did. They played their art well, they surrounded the ascetic deeply concentrated upon his self, and tried to disturb his mood of meditation by the artful display of their limbs and by all the erotic tricks of sights and glances at their command, but all in vain. The Yogi (in perfect communion with God) remained absolutely undisturbed like the deep sea full to the brim, with all his sense organs in unswerved concentration upon the highest truth. They were surprised and shocked to see the limitations of their powers. They came back to report to Indra the sad failure of their tricks. "Oh King, it is impossible to distract his mind, all our enticements have failed to attract his attention, so try a different method."

Indra saw it would not do without a direct assault. So he decided to hurl thunder, that lightning-charged fire-arm of his, to kill him. Even the mightiest should not ignore the weakest of his enemies. Thus decided Indra threw that terrific weapon upon Trisira, still completely absorbed in his thoughts of the highest truth. Thunder struck him, instantly paralysing his whole body and leaving it lifeless. But upon the countenance of the great ascetic, who had fallen like a toppled peak upon the ground, there was yet beaming a soft blissful light, which struck terror into Indra's heart. He could not look at that shining face of that great Yogi, he seemed to him more than alive, the spirit that hovered upon the body became unendurable to him. It was perhaps a psychological moment in his life. His weak mind was trying to circumvent a stronger claim to his throne by a still more corrupted means, which might not offer full satisfaction even on near success, leaving a trail of diffidence on the subconscious plane of his mind. This practically led him from crime to crime. He could not, in that unsettled state of his mind, think of sparing the latest stake of his fortune. He sought to get rid of the body itself. Chance offered him the means. A carpenter was then passing near the place with his axe upon his shoulder. Indra beckoned him on to where the dead body was and asked him to sever its head.

The carpenter told him that his axe would not be able to cut off that huge head with a shoulder of prodigious girth, moreover he would not do that cruel act. Indra, however, in an extremely obsessed state could not see the gruesomeness of the act, he was in the gasping need of it. So he encouraged him saying, "No fear, your weapon would be as strong as flint, I grant you that boon." The carpenter had no obsession, so his senses were alive to the horrid deed. He would not do it without any reason. He then asked the reason why he should do that cruel act and who he was to bid him do it. Indra, of course, said who he was, but did not give him the reason for such a provocation, the reason would have been all too despicable for words. He only asked him to do his bidding without any reservation, he should do what he was asked by no less a personality than the all-ruler of heaven. The carpenter was not, however, convinced. He held out to him the grievous side of his act. It was really shameful for one to do it, to wit to ask one to sever a dead man's head. He also drew his attention to the fact that the dead was the son of a Rishi, he was a Brahmin and surely the Indra should have been trembling at the sin of slaying a Brahmin.

Indra observed that the carpenter had raised a delicate and sensitive point and to carry his conviction he must be less in the clouds. He let him into his secrets, telling him that he had killed him with his thunder for fear, he was his rival and cause of constant worry. Also told him that he would release himself from the sin by observing the most austere course of self-purification later :

Pashchād dharmang karisyāmi pābanārthang sudurshcharam
(Ibid., 35)

He tempted him into the bargain to have share of the head of every sacrificial animal henceforth at every sacrifice man may offer. The carpenter was tempted and cut off Trisira's heads with his axe, but lo ! from the three heads three different living creatures came ! Coming out they took flight in the air as birds. We know all the details of every flight of fancy used in the epic are no use labouring too far, they are symbolic and bedecked with too many poetic fripperies. Maybe the poet was suggesting the soaring of the soul of that noble Yogi for a higher state of existence (according to the Indian conception, which is particularly emphasized in this epic, one cannot avoid existence even after physical death), and even today in various forms of poetic images the soul is comparable to the flight of birds when it leaves the body. It is very much in use in folk literature of Bengal ('soul the bird just takes its flight', for example). Trishira's body must have lain prostrate at the severe electric shock of the lightning-charged bolt hurled by Indra, but being a life-long Yogi of natural self-control he might not breathe his last breath, his body only had the look of the dead; Indra too may have had that sense and that was particularly the secret cause of his fear, he would be safe and sure of his death if only his head could be cut off from his trunk. When the head was cut off the body finally remained only a lifeless lump, his last breath left it.

(2)

Indra now thought himself relieved of the worries of his

dubious position in face of a worthier rival and wended his way to reach his palace. But he must have kept in mind that he committed a sin by so cruelly and trickily killing a Brahmin of immaculate virtue, as he was not by nature steeped in sin. What he did then is not there in the North Indian edition of the epic but in the South Indian edition. What the carpenter did is also given there, but this is not much material. Indra then took care to observe a vow in expiation of the sin. The process of expiation was unique in itself. He divided the sin of killing a Brahmin to share it with the manifested Universe, especially its four major divisions, earth, water, forest and women :

Samudresu prīthibyang cha banaspatisu strīsu cha,
Bibhajya brahmahatyāng cha tān baraibapyayojayat.

(Ibid., 44)

All spiritual communion with the highest cause, in any form, either in the form of a vow or sacrifice, in the Indian covention seeks but one ultimate effect of keeping in perpetual touch with the Universe through that Primal cause. Indra too sought that kind of spiritual realization, his sharing sins with the entire Universe, everything that is in it, by that process of psycho-physical treatment of re-establishing the already shattered powers of responses.

This made only a partial recuperation possible; every sin brings in its trail a kind of distortion on the psychic and physical planes of the being, which disturbs also the spiritual and moral order, causing impediments in the way of easy attainments and accelerated existence; any remedial process is simply contrapuntal in nature, having something to waste in the operation. Indra had to face the same situation. He countermined the hostile reactions of his already committed sin, but with some dent upon his normal power and position. The killing of Trisira did not go unexpiated. His father Rishi Tvasta, when he heard of the savage end of his son's life, sought to punish the cruel and sinful king of heaven, who had already proved himself unworthy of that high position and noble responsibility. Earlier he brought forth a human being just to match the high position of the heavenly king embodying purity and power in his self; but he was now urged by a different exigency, to bring into existence someone as a constant source of torment to the present king of heaven for revenge. The demon Britta was born out of that vengeful spirit of his father.

The birth of Trisira and of Vritta had behind them two different urges, and because of that difference their quality and character were formed different, one a boon and the other a complete bane of life. The boon was frustrated by the cruel tricks of Indra, but the bane of his life arose out of his hideous act and it would have remained a sore point even though he had expiated his sin through moral and spiritual counter courses.

By the wish of Tvasta Vritta was growing in size and strength, a prodigy of the Creation, the living curse of Indra's fate. Vritta had no personal cause to act against Indra's interest, he cannot be a worthy selection of nature for the throne of heaven, which Tvasta's other son was; he was the born enemy of heaven, his only object was to stand in constant opposition to the throne of heaven, he was instilled with that spirit of conflict from his birth. He ceremonically asked the author of his birth what he should do for him. The Rishi enjoined on him acts of enmity to the Indra of heaven. The demon began his fight in heaven, which embroiled ultimately the whole legion of gods and came to disturb peace on other planes of life too. Indra had to suffer for his sin, others too suffered with him, but not for their sins. Since sufferings were caused by the acts of Vritta, they made it a common cause with their king to fight against him. The Rishis who had also their share of bitter destiny would try to help Indra to win his war against that demon. They had no other weapons but good counsel. In his battle Indra was defeated and took temporary shelter upon the peak of Mount Mandar. The gods accompanied by the Rishis reached there to hold counsel as to how they could get rid of that pest.

Indra explained to the assembly of gods and Rishis why he fled the field to hide himself there. He was able to meet Vritta earlier, but now he did not consider himself a match for him; he was too full of vigour for him and could devour even the three worlds; so the last resort was to approach Visnu with the whole retinues to think out jointly the means of his extirpation. This diffident mood at times overpowered Indra's prowess and strength of mind. In that mood surely Indra hid himself in an unassailable region for his personal security. Now along with the Rishis and gods he came to meet Visnu and in a hymn of praise they all recounted all the past exploits which were accomplished with his imparted spirit. The revival of that dissipated energy in Indra was the need of the hour, and it is Visnu who, presiding over the whole area of responsiveness, would be the right source to mend the shattered faculty in him (Indra). This Visnu once held Indra secure upon the throne of heaven against a possible claimant, a demon Bali; he had always safeguarded the cause of the gods against that demon race; the gods and Rishis together implored him this time too to act as the mainstay of security.

Visnu would play his significant role; he assured the whole lot of this help, it was his normal duty to restore the lost values of that higher culture called heaven, but the only means to do it was to revive the already dazed moral and spiritual responses. So he suggested to the imploring assembly the path of peace, which would by itself be a weapon strong enough to repulse the assault of the strongest of demons, Vritta. Although the episode has all the appearance of a myth it has this unequivocal suggestion. Vishnu asked them to go to Britta's abode to make peace with him, which, he said, would create suitable atmosphere for his defeat. Mythologically, of course, Visnu assured them that such a deceptive climate of peace prevailing he would enter unseen into the most efficacious of weapons, thunder.

Adrishyascha prabekshyāmi bajre hyasyāyudhottame.

(Ibid., Chap. 10, 12)

Thus instructed the Rishis and gods along with Indra reached Vritta's dwelling. Vishnu knew they all reacted under the ineluctable need of self-security to the all-out assault upon peace, so they too lost sight of the true cause and its lasting remedy. A change of outlook was urgently necessary even for them. The peace proposal would bring in that change, Vishnu perhaps saw it. They approached the belligerent demon for truce. The Rishis initiated the talk : 'Oh, thou invincible, your glories fill the three worlds, thou hast not yet been able to vanquish Indra, although the fight has long been continued; the result of this prolonged war has been unending distress to all life, gods, demons and men alike. So we propose truce between you and Sakra (Indra), which will bring in an era of peace for all including yourself.'

Vritta at first doubted the effectiveness of this proposal. He told them both Indra and himself were equally powerful, and truce between two sides of identical strength would not last long. The Rishis at this pleaded a noble cause of virtue, a contact with the virtuous even for once would be desirable, they aggrandized Indra as the foremost of the virtuous and respected by them all. They showered praises of all sorts, not all strictly well-deserved, but deliberately calculated to their purpose. So one cannot say they were irrelevant, in all their prevarications and truisms they maintained essential verities :

Sakrit satāng sangatang lipsitabyang
Tatah parang bhabitā bhabyameba.

(Ibid., 23)

The significant word used by them was Bhabita, the ineluctable law, which must take its course. True it is, neither Indra nor the demon Vritta could dodge the destiny they had made out of their acts.

However, the demon who derived something out of his paternal instinct had great respect for the meritorious Rishis. He agreed to their proposal, but took some precautionary step, because he could not rely upon the integrity of the dissembling Indra. He wanted Indra and all other gods to bind themselves to the agreement that they should not kill him with anything either dry or wet, nor with stone or wood, nor with a handy weapon or a missile, nor even by day or at night either. He laid his trust in the Rishis, and would honour their appeal, but the gods must before that accept this agreement; and the articles of agreement were so carefully formulated that they practically left no scope for their betrayal, at least Vritta thought so. The Rishis interceded for Indra to accept his terms, which led the demon to rejoice in sight of the security of his life.

The Rishis did not want any harm to anybody, neither to Indra nor to his enemy Vritta, they wanted peace, and they acted their role as peacemaker between them. But Indra was not of their mind and temperament. The peace that was concluded thereby gave no respite from the tension of his mind. He was always afraid of a rival Indra; to seek relief from such a claimant he had committed a grisly murder, really a meritorious Yogi who never deserved a comminatory vengeance like that. This time he had rather sufficient cause to be stirred against a demon who had done much harm to the interest personally of his own and the whole culture of heaven. So even after truce being made he could not rest sure of his position, he was thinking of any means of quick despatch of his rival's life. Particularly when he saw Vritta moving with full vigour on the beach of the ocean just in the twilight of sunset it sored his mind as it were like a sharp cut. He thought, "This is the time when a death blow to Vritta will not perhaps falsify the assurance given to him by the godly Rishis; on the other hand if I do not take this opportunity and spare him it will darken all my future." So thinking Indra got to weigh the pros and cons of the whole matter. It was twilight, neither day nor night, then it was Vishnu who gave him undertaking to help kill Vritta, but how ? While scanning like that in his mind it came into view a huge mountain of surf with a crest of white foam. At once it struck him that this frothy peak was neither dry nor wet, nor could it be considered a weapon. He at once decided to strike Britta with that improvised instrument of death in which he must have concealed his deadly weapon thunder and invoked the spirit of Vishnu to his aid.

Sabajramatha phenang tang kshiprang Britre nisristabān
Prabishya phenang tang Bisnuratha Britrang byanāshayat.
(Ibid., 39)

By the very mythical style of the epic the above verse may well construe Indra's very astute method of hitting the enemy at his most relaxed and disarmed state, it might compare with the very pre-emptive attack of modern warfare. Vishnu's assurance of help he must have utilized as a moral force to cover up his wicked means. However he had thus got rid of his greatest enemy, and served his personal interest, and only obliquely served a general interest of peace and prosperity to all the rest. The whole community of gods and Rishis heaved a sigh of relief and rejoiced at the success of Indra, the well-meaning Rishis, of course, did not want to have it done in this way, but wanted peace from the very inmost heart of their hearts so much eagerly that they did not at all care how it came about. This perhaps set the stage for another unforeseen reversal in the course of events in the near future.

The victory was celebrated by high and low all, the gods, Rishis, the people of the earth and even all lower grades of the Creation; Indra was adored and accosted by the elite among his subjects and led to the throne with all ceremonial grandeur. Indra too worshipped Vishnu in company with other gods of heaven in humble submission to his great power. When things were thus settled and he was quite out of his funk Indra got into a morbid sombre mood, the outward peace led him into a sort of soul-searching. The Rishis of the highest moral sense would have also got behind the whole operation that ultimately gave them this peace. Perhaps their early enthusiasm for peace was by then subsided to a cold analysis of the moral and spiritual basis of Indra's victory. So within a very short period of time both externally and internally, among the leading members of the subjects and in the mind of the heaven ruler himself, the air of mirth and self-satisfaction was replaced by a sordid self-deception. This perhaps led to Indra's sudden and almost unaccountable disappearance from heaven. The epic has not given any elaborate details of Indra's flight, and no doubt with perfect artistic cogency.

Just seated steady upon the throne of heaven Indra was in a sort of mental brooding, in which all his past activities cast their lurid shadows, really a secret half-conscious operation of the mind only deepened by an external air of coldness besetting him. The epic has rightly spotlighted the end view without going for the cold-blooded psychological analysis. While Indra was plodding through the whole seminary of past activities, two particular events of his life must have loomed very large, the epic has only touched upon them, and pinned down one of them for special emphasis, that very criminal act of killing a Brahmin, Trisira.

Tato hate mahābīrye Britre debabhayankare.
Anritenābhibhūtoabhuchchhakrah paramadurmanāh
Traishīrsayabhibhūtashcha sa purbang brahmahatyayā.

(Ibid., 43-44)

He was then addle-brained to think of the murder of Trisira, a Brahmin, and was irretrievably overpowered by a sense of sin in his lachrymose mood, when he had already done with the life of Vritta. It is the murder of Trisira that caused a wholesale dislocation of his mental faculties, he could not face it and out of deep remorse left the throne for which he committed that macabre crime. This is the beginning of the next phase of his life.

THE MYSTERY AROUND THE BIRTH OF THE BASUS

The Mahabharata episode of the birth of Bhisma demonstrates a scientific eugenic process drawing into its operation some typical mythical characters with all the grandeur of the epic style. The truth behind the imposing superstructure is the ulterior end of the epic, and the present essay's too.

(1)

The Mahabharata narrates the story of an assembly of gods before the Supreme Ordainer, Brahma, where one of the Ikshaku kings was found. Why he was there the text has clearly given it. In the Indian tradition of the Aryan stage man's evolution in a cycle of births was an accepted truth and in the estimation of man the intangible stages of his past and future were taken up with the tangible human stage, and the highest state in existence was attainment of divinity. Man can either rise to that state or fall from it. This total view of man's evolution gave all the spur to the spiritual orientation and the stylistic innovation of the great epic. The Ikshaku king Mahabhish by dint of his kingly sacrifices attained to that heavenly bliss and was among the gods in presence of Brahma. This is how he evolved into that desired state. The epic has considered how he fell from it.

One of the goddesses, Ganga, came also into the presence of the Great Grandfather of the whole creation as Brahma is called. She came all on a sudden and must have caused a stir there among the gods, quite natural, a lady of celestial beauty tripping there to add an uncommon lustre to the scene. The lady when she appeared sufficiently careful about the adjustment of her garments, only a gust of wind blew her clothings up to leave her body quite naked and bare.

Tasyā bāsah samuddhūtang mārutena shashiprabhang

(Adi Parba, Chap. 96, 4)

When such an unexpected discomfiture arose, the members of the assembly reacted, betraying their respective elements. They sat there with their eyes downcast to spare the divine lady inescapable embarrassment, but king Mahabhish who attained heaven by the merit of his deeds could not restrain his unseemly temptation for a sly scrutiny of the uncovered parts of the lady's body. He did it unscared by the goddess's reaction : her reaction was rather inviting to him. He managed to escape other gods' notice, there was cause to do so, they all behaved with a different taste, sharply contrasted with his. But the goddess who was directly involved in the case gave sign of an ungodly taste. She neither remained indifferent to the lustful leer and side-glances of the king nor could discourage him with a repulsive grimace. Really the goddess meant neither of the courses. She practically encouraged the king by an equally lusty glance askance. And not only that, she was quite impressed by the king's responses to a sort of physical temptation, which she may not have all too unwarily offered. Is it not next to impossible for the wind, however strong, to blow up almost the whole of the lady's lower garments, if she had not been rather carefully careless about it ? The lady passed near the king just thinking of him in the depth of her mind, perhaps a little rapturously. Let us follow the text :

Mahābhisastu rājarsirashanko dritabān nadīm.

(Ibid., 5)

* * * *

Mahābhisang tu tang dristvā nadī dhaiyachchutang nripang
Tameba manasā dhyāyantyupābartat saridvarā

(Ibid., 9, 10)

The stir and awakening in both are quite suggestive of their future prospect. No separate rules are there in nature for gods and a different set for men, they were rather governed by the same principles of life, with a prospect of upward and downward trend in evolution just in the right proportion to the choice made. The earth-born king and the heaven-born goddess were inseparably tied together in the spiritual depth of their relationship. Originally they were not related, unless by the inevitability of that ultimate source of our origin. But they became spiritually so inextricably knit together by their mutual emotional reactions that it ordained their future stage in evolution. The symbolic representation of the disinterested ordainer of principles, Brahma, called the Grandfather of the whole creation, took note of these reactions in them and suggested inescapable consequence in the form of a warning of curse, rightly merited by their courses of action :

Soapadhyāto bhagabatā brahmanā tu mahābhisah
Uktashcha jāto martyesu punarlokānabāpsyasi.
Yathāpahritamanāshchāsi gangayā tvang hi durmate,
Sā te bai mānuse loke bipriyānyācharisyati.
Yadā te bhabitā manyustadā shāpād bimokshyase.

(Ibid., 6-8)

Brahma marked this reaction in Mahabhish and suspected him and then said that since his mind was quite engrossed in the thought of Ganga and infected thereby, he would be born in the mortal world again, and she too in that human existence would do his pleasure and he would thereafter be released from this curse just exalted in mind from contentment.

(2)

Brahma has only suggested through his curse an inevitably evolved stage of the relationship between Ganga and Mahabhish, which they only started by their mutual rapturous liking. They have established the basis of their human relationship as between the two opposite sexes, they are to be born one for the other to make it possible for an elevated normal evolution to the highest goal of human life. They are involved in an inseverable spiritual affinity.

Now the question is where would they be born and how should they come together. In Indian tradition of culture nothing is altogether unrelated to anything else. One cause is another's effect, and the effect is again the cause of a still remoter effect, as a link in an endless chain of reactions. So their birth, union and parenthood are not unrelated phenomena in the wider perspective of a moral order, they are linked with possible other inevitabilities.

The story of the birth of the Basus is linked with this evolution. The king thought, of course, who could be his father in the next birth ? His mind ran after the celebrated king Pratipa in the Iksaku line. So it was destined he should be born in the same family as the son of king Pratipa. Pratipa, too, on his own side was in eager expectation of a son, the exigency arose from his apparently chance meeting with Ganga at the time of his observance of a meritorious vow. While Pratipa was doing the rites of his penance on the bank of the river Ganga, a lady of resplendent beauty, the embodiment of the river itself, approached him for the gratification of her womanly desire, practically she sat upon the right knee of the king then absorbed in meditation. The king wished her good but could not accept this offer, he told her directly that he was under a vow, which ruled out all such act of enjoyment of the purely physical and sensual nature, with a woman already espoused to another. The king, however, found it difficult to dissuade the lady who had peremptorily took her position upon one of his knees and was well-versed in all the postulates of Dharma and the edicts of the man and woman relations. So the king assured her that her offer would be reserved for his son yet unborn, and gave her also to understand that she had perchance ensured this future course by her very choice, a lady who may choose to sit upon the right knee instead of the left is only worthy to be a daughter-in-law, son's wife, according to the principles of etiquette. The lady was then persuaded and would wait for the king's son.

The lady's destiny which was already ordained by her own nature and behaviour fulfils itself through the related destinies overruling others' lives. Mahabhish is now going to be born to king Pratipa, which was also enforced by another inviolable exigency in the life of the cursed Basus. The divine lady Ganga, while coming out of the presence of Brahma, met in the way in their shattered health the deformed Basus. She asked them the reasons of such a faded glory and misery. They retorted they were under a curse for no great offence to the Rishi Bashista. Although the consequence of the curse remains the same, the reasons behind show some variations in the text of the Mahabharata. This is, of course, in the very spirit of the epic style. The Basus were cursed by the Rishi, they did no proper homage to him in his unimpressive attire as a commoner. But when Ganga herself narrated the reason to his earthly husband it became an altogether different story, and it is more in harmony with the moral order.

In the second account the Basus accompanied by their wives came to the hermitage of Bashista, where they saw the divine cow Nandini by name and learnt her special merit. Her milk could perpetuate one's youth and vigour for many years to come, here mythically ten thousand years. When the wife of one of the Basus named Dyu learnt it she asked her husband to take away the cow for her girl-friend, Jitabati, on earth, famed for her all-surpassing beauty. She would have her friend, as Shakespeare wished in his Sonnets, enjoy unfading beauty for her pleasure and the pleasure of the world by means of the cow's milk. Dyu was so very ensnared by his affection for his wife that he was irretrievably instigated, quite heedless of the justness of his act, to steal away the cow and her calf to satisfy his wife's humour. He took help of all his brothers in the act of stealing. This was a wrong done to the Rishi, just slighting his merit and power. May be it was metaphorically represented in the earlier account given by the Basus themselves, a sort of slight for the respectable person of the Rishi.

The imprecations were not, however, unmerited. The Basus were to be born human and on earth, but they required worthy parents for their human birth. So they implored Ganga, who was lately under the moral exigency to be born human forfeiting her godly state of bliss, to ensure their birth and hurry their release from that anathema and restoration to their original divine majesty.

Thus it seems to be an enforced coincidence that king Mahabhish would be born as king Pratipa's son to be espoused to Ganga and the Basus would take the opportunity to be born to their union. Natural selection and destiny as an indispensable part of the moral order when recounted in human terms within the short and very limited compass of our knowledge appear to be a little contrived, taken out of thousand other unknown and unaccounted sequences, which taken together come properly to be called consequence. Even in the mythical grandeur of an epic like the Mahabharata such an impression is almost inescapable. But the epic culture of India enforces the idea that consequence is the sum total of things in their perfect sequence. The whole story of the birth of the Basus is arranged in the pages of the epic to give that impression.

(3)

King Pratipa was impatiently awaiting the birth of a son even in his old age for the promise he made to that entreating lady. Then in course of time to that old pair a son was born, it was Mahabhish who was born as their son under a new name, Santanu, because of his being born of the royal pair in their contented state of mind from observance of sacrificial rites :

Tayoh samabhabat putro briddhayoh sa mahābhisah
Shāntasya jajne sangtānastasmadāsīt sah shāntanuh

(Ibid., Chap. 97, 18-19)

King Pratipa did not forget his pledge to the divine lady. So he communicated to his son who came of age for such a confidence. He gave him his entire story about the lady. She came to him once, he told him, to give birth to him by him. But it is not ordained that he should be born of her, their encounter in the previous birth destined them to be man and wife. Pratipa, of course, did not know it, but the turn of his mind unknowingly fulfilled that prospect. He asked his son not to frustrate the approach of a lady of such quality and character as he met in the prime of his life for any prudish notion of propriety, but to honour her legitimate appeal for gratification of her desire to be the mother of his children. He also warned him not to disregard any of her desire after their union.

Santanu did not know how the die of his destiny was cast. His father only half-unknowingly spread the board. He came to the throne of his father and developed a charming young man indulging in all youthful pastimes like roaming and hunting. In one such exploit he passed near the river Ganga when all at once he found a super-excellent beauty, moving as it were like the concentrated glory of her sex, with her maddening fascination of her body. It is the same lady as met his father once for satisfaction of her womanly desire and was put away ever since discontented perhaps till this occasion, a just opportunity for the unfulfilled desire to be fulfilled. The youthful king too was waiting his chance, in this birth, of satisfaction of a roused passion in the earlier. So the young hero's response was immediate and irrevocably decided. The movements of both of them are simply a further step from the earlier meeting. The text of the epic has carefully recorded it :

Tāng dristvā hristaromābhūd bismito rūpasampadā,
Pibanniba cha netrābhyāng nātripyata narādaipah.
Sā cha dristveba rājānang bicharantang mahādvutim,
Snehādāgatasauhārdā nātripyata bilāsinī.

(Ibid., 29-30)

They made no secret of their already awakened love for each other. This time they had no reason to be restrained by the eyes of others, nor had they any scruples of the earlier birth. They exchanged their minds, the feelings of their hearts, firstly by no words of their mouth, but by the mute gesture of their limbs and the tremulous light of their eyes. Then the king came to the state of articulation of his passion. The lady accepted the offer, she was inwardly after this end, but forbore to pronounce it in clear terms, she had yet some trust to fulfil by means of her union. However strongly she felt in her heart the force of passion her sense of responsibility was not beclouded. So she dictated her terms for acceptance of the king's offer, knowing quite well that he would not disoblige her. She set her conditions of complete freedom in her relationship with her husband, the king had no idea that it would extend up to their conjugal relationship governing even the sex-life. He was too completely overpowered by passion to deny it. Besides he recollected his father's warning. She set forth her terms in the following words :

Yat tu kuryāmahang rājanchhubhang bā yadi bāshubham
Na tad bārayitabyāsmi na baktabyā tathāpriyam

(Ibid., Chap. 98, 3)

She is ensured absolute freedom of action and will. Now the question is why she insisted upon this freedom and what use she did make of it ? To make a cryptic answer, she remembered the pledge to the luckless Basus, and even in her conjugal life and all her life of pleasure she would shape things in such a manner as to make their earthly birth possible. There remains the true essence of the institution of marriage, a perfect synthesis of a natural bodily need, call it pleasure of the flesh if you like, and a spiritual purpose—a natural harmony between pleasure and purpose.

The elegant lady lived with Santanu to the utmost happiness of the latter. But in the course of the happy life together some subdued undertone of disharmony came to rule their conjugal relationship. The king could not take it aright that their sexual relationship too would be dictated by the wife, he thought it to be a kind of unnecessary and unnatural female domination, even the behaviour of the wife after the birth of their children seemed to him abnormally cruel. Although he was vowed to ungrudging submission to her wishes he could not conciliate his mind to all her wanton activities. In the text the waywardness of the lady is given its utmost edge. When a son was born to them Ganga threw it immedietely into the water of the river. The king's infatuation with his queen was so great that he hazarded no question, lest she might leave him. The queen thus threw as many as seven children into the river one after another immediately after their birth, and at the time of the eighth the king challenged the queen's brutal course. The queen did not, of course, throw this son born to them, perhaps she would not have done it of her own; now because of the very act of non-compliance with the terms Ganga decided to leave him, first explaining her behaviour to him. She narrated in full the story of the Basus' misadventure at the hermitage of the Sage Bashista and the crucial role of the last of the Basus. The Rishi, while pronouncing the curse, made a distinction between the role of the last one and that of the rest. It was Dyu who took it into his head to steal away the divine cow persuaded by his wife for the benefit of her earthly girl friend—a great breach for a flimsy cause. Not only that it was he who made all his brothers accomplices of his misdeeds. So his punishment was the heaviest, under the Sage's imprecations he would have to lead his life on earth, never a married man, as his married wife led him astray from the right path into the path of sin. And the other brothers who only helped him in his desparate act would only be born on earth to be immediately released from the curse's effect. Ganga explained to her earthly consort that she had only fulfilled the already destined course. The last born son would remain his father's son, a peerless hero deprived of all the bliss of married love.

(4)

The wanton acts of Ganga are all within the framework of a preordained formula, one knows. Her marriage with the king is also destined by the ordinary impulses of her life in a previous birth as also by the reactions in the life of the other party heretofore. But one thing still remains to be fully clarified why Ganga imposed some conditions of her free choice even in matters of sexual engagement with her husband. When she sought to be assured of absolute freedom in everything in relation to her lord, she must have meant particularly sexual union, which the king at first may not anticipate. She especially meant it because it was indispensably related to that noble trust of the Basus.

Marital relation according to the ancient Indian view is first a psychological and even spiritual selection and then material and physical fulfilment, both are in an inevitable sequence; if this psychological involvement is ignored or not scientifically adjusted trails of distorted moral twist are the unavoidable result. That adjustment in the form of an inevitability in the Ganga-Mahabhish relation is sought here. Besides, the procreation process is conditioned by the female-initiative, so in Indian acceptation a mother is called Mata, one who measures up the issue in its essential prospect. This eugenic science must have been known to ancient Indian women, at least women like Ganga's attainments. She assured the Basus that she would bear her children with the already stipulated possibility. To measure them to the right size as they had desired, and to bring forth only those, required on her part an emotional trimming of the right measure, to inspire withal the generative machinery, to use a scientific expression, in the male party. Naturally such emotional concentration cannot always be kept up; when such a rare moment as that is warmed up and fully realized, surely that is the exquisite point for procreative participation of husband and wife for the exalted and concentrated passion to be embodied in a new being. This is the reason why Ganga reserved the unquestioned right of sexual union with her husband, fully to exploit the moment of that emotional attainment. Thus she bore all of them and got seven of them as shortlived on earth as they desired, she measured them up so by an exacting desire of her own at the time of union. Similarly she got the eighth son emotionally conceived as long-lived and as incontinent as the Rishi had determined him to be on earth at the time of its begetting. The Rishi's curse was fulfilled, but not unscientifically and out of moral sequence. The king too must have been, after the death of all the seven sons in succession, emotionally in harmony with his wife to have the last son's longevity considerably extended and his mental outlook a good deal elevated, in fact by the exaltation of his mood, exactly timed with the exalted mood of his wife.

The king's earnestness is demonstrated by an oblique turn of his mood just after the birth of this child, he would not allow his wife to throw it into the water, really she would not have to, the child had already been conceived mentally and physically quite otherwise. The very treatment of life's principles in the Mahabharata is stylistically interesting in this respect. It conceals the truth in the warp and woof of fancy. Their conjugal squabbles after the child's birth are only a conscious reaction to an unconsciously established unity of urge at its conception.

Now after a quarrel husband and wife parted, that is also according to the terms and conditions governing their union. The king is left with the newly born son in whom the future prospect is rightly destined by the wanton acts of his earlier birth. The excessive uxoriousness which blinded him to the wrong he committed to the Rishi, by depriving him of his well-deserved possession, did him an irreparable damage frustrating his rightful possession of a wife, the wife who proved to him more than the path of virtue. His atonement did not end here, in his present birth as Bhisma he would also be deprived of the comforts of the throne. He is given to lead a life of constant sacrifice in this birth although within the scope of a Kshatriya profession, his birth-right in this life. So Bhisma is not only an incomparable hero but also a receptacle of vast knowledge of scripture.

(5)

The divine lady Ganga was no doubt passionate, her very appearance in the assembly of gods with amorous carelessness of clothes is evidence enough. But she fulfilled a higher purpose by her passion through her married life. In the service of that higher ideal she must have attained an exalted mood, making passion itself only a secondary concern. This may have caused her stay at the king's palace after the birth of the last of the Basus to turn a banal experience. So she left the palace. The king too without her found life charmless, and wanted to create a new charm of spiritual merit in stead. So he left the palace to pursue a course of forty years' asceticism in a secluded place. The son by this time became a lusty young man taught all the principles of Dharma by the Sage Bashista. When the king saw his own son after years of absence by the river side he could not recognize immediately that he was his son grown so elegant with the beauty of his body and mind. The already parted wife Ganga had to recall to the king's mind his early memories and introduce the young man as their own. The king then would do his father's duty by the son, ceremonially declared him as the Prince, heir to the throne, at the palace.

At this juncture of events something happened to the still conjugally unsatisfied king. Ganga played a part in his life, but that went particularly to serve a purpose the lady nobly undertook to accomplish in her own married life. So the king's desire which was really roused by the sight of the lady's unrobed body unconsciously sought to be satisfied, even though he tried to adjust it to a higher spiritual attainment. The king spent four years with his son, no doubt ruling the country from the capital and taking no particular care to reinforce spiritual exaltation in life. Hence a relapse into a desire for worldly pleasure. This is indicated by the king's taking a fancy to a beautiful lady of a working class while paying a visit to another river, the Yamuna. He was first attracted by a kind of enchanting smell, the scent of the lady's body. The maddening beauty of the maiden stole upon the mind and heart of the king, there would be no happiness in his life without the girl, he thought, although he found that the girl was born of a professional class and paddled her father's canoe for her father. But he so completely abandoned himself to passion that he took no other factors into consideration than her beauty and approached the father with a formal offer of marriage. The father who was a monarch in his profession carefully considered the king's domestic affairs and the future of his daughter in the palace intrigue of succession, and sought categorical assurance of the undisputed claim of his daughter's issue to the throne. The king could not immediately commit himself to these unjust terms of marriage, but he felt not the least released from the obsessive desire for that. He returned to the capital utterly disconsolate and gone far deep into his desire for the maid.

Sa chintayanneba tadā dāshakanyāng mahipatih,
Pratyayāddhastināpurang kāmopahatachetanah.

(Ibid., Chap. 100, 58)

His unrealised desire gradually preyed upon his mind and body and completely dilapidated his health even without any known cause or disease. So one day this was remarked by his son, then called Debabrata, and the king's answer was partly shaded and partly sincere. He could not confide to his son the whole truth, he gave it a religious colour. He told him that a father of one son only is considered spiritually as a father without any issue, so for him there would be no heavenly bliss in the life after. The son, of course, confidentially learnt the true cause of his father's ruined health from the Minister. He was passing his agonized existence for not been able to marry the daughter of the best of the fisherman community, particularly owing to the preconditions set forth by the father. The great hero Debabrata then approached the king of the fishermen on his father's behalf, accepted the conditions he put forward for the marriage of his daughter, and conceded also to a further condition that the throne must be reserved for the posterity in his daughter's line. Debabrata then agreed to forego the throne himself and was pledged to perpetual celibacy, so that all obstacles were removed from his father's marriage to the daughter. Overwhelmed by the sacrifice his son made for the gratification of his desire Santanu blessed his son with a boon of death at will and changed his mame to Bhisma, considering the severity of his pledge.

The story is very simple, but it illustrates in usual mythological style a truth how destiny works through human agencies, sometimes through mental reactions of an extremely elusive kind, and how in its operation destiny covers a wider area of several births. The chance or arbitrary orientation of human decisions only appear to be so when unconnected with their germs in the earlier stages, or else nothing is arbitrary in the Universe, rather in a perfect sequence of inevitability, only invisible and imperceptible to a surface view. The decision made by Bhisma under the exigencies of the external pressures is neither unrelated nor unmerited, rather caused by a moral order of reactions of all our choices in a remote plane.

KRISHNA'S LESSON ON TRUTH AND DHARMA

Krishna has offered lesson on the controversial issue of a choice between the two alternatives that appear confusive to the warrior Arjuna as he did on another occasion. Both these occasions occur in the battlefield, but Krishna's dictation on Dharma just at a moment of bewilderment in which Arjuna found himself before the fighting began was on a general line of ethical principles. In the present article a definite intervention by his Lordship with specific examples and explications to clear the idea of truth to Arjuna is taken up for elaboration.

(1)

Arjuna rushed through the thick of the field to seek for Yudhisthira, so was he advised by Lord Krishna : but nowhere could he find his brother, and perhaps hardly could he find him if he were not directed by Krishna himself to where the tired and exhausted brother retreated for respite from the bitterest assaults upon his army by the Kaurava general Karna. The text in the epic records why Krishna advised Arjuna to avoid Karna in the first fury of his onslaught; he did not explain his strategy to Arjuna, but only let it work in a designed withdrawal from battle. Arjuna drove to the secret retreat of Yudhisthira, the hiding place was, however, not within his knowledge, only Lord Krishna knew and he led him there, a distance of two miles from the battlefield.

The meeting between these two brothers is very dramatic. Arjuna saw Yudhisthira in the last stage of fatigue and terribly excited, and Yudhisthira saw both Arjuna and Krishna blood-stained all over because of innumerable scars of arrows upon their bodies. Yudhisthira retreated to that secluded corner from the field, defeated by the army under Karna's command, injured bodily and disspirited by the entire success of their thrust upon them. The terror of Karna's assault so fully gripped his mind that he was led into an illusion of total massacre of Karna and his army which Arjuna with the divine pilot to lead him must have wrought.

Yudhisthira accosted Krishna and Arjuna with the story of Karna whom he had taken to have been already killed. Arjuna, he thought, earned the fame of killing that invincible enemy. It is rather a wish-fulfilment for Yudhisthira to think like that. Karna had ever remained the object of envy, there may have been some unconscious instinctive rivalry for the claim of Kunti's first-born, the episode of Karna's birth seems to have been still unknown to him. In a moment of nightmarish excitement after an ignoble defeat all his latent horror of Karna assumed menacingly telling forms. He confessed how terribly disturbed he remained all the thirteen years, day in and day out, for fear of Karna, and that he could not enjoy even a wink of sleep, nor felt happy any moment of his life.

Jāgratsvapanangshcha Kounteya sadā hyaham,
Pashyāmi tatra tatraiba Karnabhūtamidang jagat.
Yatra yatra gachchhami Karnāt bhīto Dhanangjaya,
Tatra tatra hi pashyāmi Karnamebāgratah sthitam.
(Karna Parba, Chap. 75, 18-19)

Whether awake or asleep, wherever he went, Yudhisthira told Arjuna, he saw Karna as if the whole world were filled with him; wherever he fled for fear of Karna he saw him leading ahead always.

Yudhisthira wished his death, and thought his wish fulfilled at the sudden appearance of Krishna and Arjuna at once. He narrated all the misdeeds of Karna from his tormented memory, particularly those acts of his which oppressed him most and remained ever since as unhealed scars upon his mind. One such wound was his vaunting words regarding Draupadi. He reminded Arjuna how Karna instigated Dushasana to haul her down to the court by main force with leering eyes and a beaming face. It was he who told Krishna (Draupadi) in presence of the Kauravas why she did not yet shun company of the weak and wretched Pandavas. He then wanted to know how Arjuna had despatched such a wicked demon, it would be the highest satisfaction for him to have the process of killing rehearsed.

Yudhisthira was so obsessed with the thought of Karna's killing that he could not once think of his remaining alive, and so he got extremely infuriated when Arjuna narrated otherwise. He related to him the terrible fight which he gave to Asvathama, the son of his war-instructor. And then Karna came to Asvathama's defence when the whole of his army was routed by Arjuna, he came dealing a terrible thrust, which Lord Krishna ordered Arjuna to avoid. They came first to meet Yudhisthira and asked him to witness personally how Karna would die in the battle they would give him presently. To learn anew what he least expected or what was diametrically opposed to his already confirmed notion or illusion is not only a terrible shock to Yudhisthira but also at the same time totally shattering to his happy dream. The result was a psychological violence in him presently wreaked upon Arjuna when he found no one else near. While giving vent to his fury Yudhisthira could not let sleep his complexes, rather let them raise their serpent's head in the sub-conscious regions of his mind and let loose upon his heroic brother. Of course all these arose from Yudhisthira's fear-psychosis, which did no further wrong than incite him by expostulation, a little too unbearable to Arjuna. Yudhisthira alleged he must have fled for fear of Karna and left Bhima alone to bear the brunt of the fierce assault by the enemy. He uttered even harsher reproaches than this : He told Arjuna that he had better run to waste in noble Kunti's womb by a five month miscarriage than fly the field in that manner; he asked him to release his bow and arrow to Basudeva who would pay proper respect to it by slaying Karna.

This last injunction enraged Arjuna beyond all bounds. He drew his sword at Yudhisthira, apparently an inhuman and inordinate gesture on the part of a quite obedient younger brother. It would have taken a tragic turn but for the timely intervention of Lord Krishna. Krishna knowing the secret reason too well asked Arjuna, as though he was quite ignorant, why he brandished his sabre although not in presence of any adversary. Arjuna explained that he had a secret vow to slay him who may have done the injury to his fame to ask him to part with his personal weapon, Gandiba by name, for an abler hand. Yudhisthira had done it and it would be a violation of truth not to slay him. Normally Arjuna did not want to kill a dear brother, but it was now bound by truth itself. He asked Krishna's view and was well-disposed to submit to his instruction in this regard.

(2)

Lord Krishna explored in this connection the whole ethics of truth for Arjuna's enlightenment about his just course of action. He started with a bitter reproach and exordium of his specific approach to this case. He told Arjuna how improper it was for him to wish to kill an elder brother of high repute and immense knowledge of Dharma for a misconceived truth. He ought to have known the comparative merit of life and truth. One should not misprize life for an undue insistence on truth, one may even fall back upon untruth rather than take to violence, Lord Krishna made it clear :

Anritāng bā baded bāchang na tu hingsyāt kathangchana

(Ibid., Chap. 69, 23)

Arjuna has, contrary to the edicts of true religion, gone to slay one unengaged in combat, and, grievously one who deserves his respect and unqualified allegiance. Lord Krishna would quote authority to explain Dharma to Arjuna. He knew it would be repellent to the audience and defeat the whole purpose if he imposed his own authority, which he was in the ultimate analysis, embodying the essential principle of Dharma in its entirety. So he referred it to the Kaurava grandfather Bhisma, Yudhisthira, Vidura and the famed Kunti as authority of Dharma, and proposed to analyse it after them.

He starts with a pointed assertion about the extreme difficulty of making distinction between truth and falsehood. One should tell a lie rather than speak the truth where the truth is more like a lie and the lie is more than a truth.

Bhabet satyamabaktabyang baktabyamanritang bhabet,
Yatrānritang bhabet satyang satyang chāpyanritang bhabet.

(Ibid., 32)

Only that man is conversed with the secrets of Dharma who knows the distinction between truth and falsehood, Lord Krishna told Arjuna and pointed out cases where lie is not incriminating—marriage, sexual engagement, loss of life, loss of one's all and the security of a Brahmin (one attaining the knowledge of the cause of the Universe). Lie used for fun which is neither right nor wrong is better called white lie, but lie for security of life and wealth and safety of particularly one who could render immense good by his very existence is more valued than factual accuracy, Krishna may have suggested it in his aphoristic pronouncement. Every act of Dharma has got behind it the urgency of life, life is the ultimate source of inspiration for all the stipulations of Dharma.

Lord Krishna with his characteristic self-negation draws an episode of mythology to further explain his point. He referred to the Balak-Kaushik story already known in Indian myths. A fowler called Balak earned the merit of truth by even an act of utmost cruelty and a pious-minded Brahmin named Kaushik invited the perdition of hell by a seemingly meritorious act of truth. Lord Krishna narrated the story which runs its long meandering course in conformity with the epic style. Here it is sought to be represented in as short a compass as possible.

The fowler hunted animals only for his elderly parents, and wife and children, whom he took under his care and protection. One day when he nowhere found any game for hunting he killed a nice-looking one-eyed wild animal while it was eagerly drinking water. This creature had a special power of scenting the tracks of its preys, so blessed with a special power of destruction derived out of a meritorious boon. Only to limit the scope of destructivity God sent a blight upon its eye. Strange it is to notice celestial vehicle to touch down the earth to fly the hunter up to heaven amidst a shower of flowers. He reached heaven by ridding the forest of the bane of life the beast surely proved to be. The pious Brahmin, Kaushik, on the other hand spoke the truth to a horde of bandits in the forest, practically helping them to track down a fleeing band of victims, fleeing for life. The Brahmin went to hell for this grievous sin, the sin he committed by disclosing the fact misjudged as truth-telling.

From both these examples one may clearly derive the essence of Dharma, of which truth is an indispensable factor. Truth cannot counteract or contradict life and its acceleration, rather it has only to serve the principle of life and evolution in whichever form it can, - even in apparent contradiction. Lord Krishna then taught Arjuna the process of evolution of Dharma itself. The principles of Dharma are enunciated in the Vedas, but Lord Krishna told him that the enunciation may not be an exhaustive record, because the true origin of Dharma is not, and cannot be, a recorded testament, the origin lies in the progress of life itself. Life is as old as creation itself and as infinite as the march of Time. So is Dharma which cannot be confined to recorded stipulations. So man must be guided by the implications of life. Lord Krishna has suggested it in his elaboration and has eventually offered the definition of Dharma :

Prabhabārthāya bhūtānāng dharmaprabachanang kritang.
Yat syāt ahingsāyuktang sa dharma iti nishchayah
Ahingsārthāya bhūtānāng dharmaprabachanang kritang
Dhāranāt dharmamityāhudharmo dhārayate prajāh
Yat syāt dhāranasangyuktang sa dharma iti nirchayah,

(Ibid., 57-58.)

Stipulations of Dharma were made for the acceleration of life, Dharma is what is steeped in non-violence to it, for non-violence to life all the enunciations of Dharma were evolved; from this upholding capability it is called Dharma, that which sustains all the living beings to existence, anything with this inspiriting merit is termed Dharma.

In the light of this interpretation of Dharma truth-telling may even turn grievous sin, as it has in the case of Kaushika who became the cause of death to a host of innocent travellers. Lord Krishna suggested by implication what he should have done, if one comes to ask for another's whereabouts to take his life it is Dharma to observe silence about his movements if it is known at all, and if, in any case, one is to speak he must not speak the truth, there lie is Dharma that serves life. After all these elaborations Krishna asked Arjuna to consider on his own whether Yudhisthira his brother was worth-killing.

(3)

Arjuna weighed both the sides of the issue and came to the conclusion that he could not slay his brother, although his pledge required it. He had already contracted sin by wishing to kill a brother, which, of course, must have been from obsession. Arjuna admitted it and asked for a method of fulfilling both his stakes. Arjuna could understand Krishna's interpretation of Dharma, but could not yet get rid of his personal notion, so he thought of some method which could be the best compromise between them. Lord Krishna had ultimately to respond to this inquiry. He first started with an explanation of the background of circumstances which caused the righteous Yudhisthira to pronounce curse upon him. Yudhisthira retreated from the field under extreme duress, tormented both in body and mind by innumerable scars of weapons all over his body in the terrible onslaught of the army under Karna. So in his utmost anxiety and anger he had inveighed against Arjuna, virtually to incite him to action against Karna. Krishna told him the ultimate meaning of Yudhisthira's reproach, so it was no case of real imprecation, Arjuna could very well ignore it and act upon the brother's true intention. Yet if he at all wanted fulfilment of his pledge Krishna would suggest alternative method as he desired. He asked Arjuna to make an ignominous address to Yudhisthira to prove him dead when alive, ignominy is equivalent to death to a man of respect; he advised him to address the respectable brother as 'you fellow', he quoted the Vedas in support of his instruction. He suggested also how to mend it afterwards, and finally inspired him to fight Karna down as the true intention of Yudhisthira was.

According to Lord Krishna's instruction Arjuna addressed Yudhisthira disrespectfully and in his reproachful address there must have been some reflections of his obsessive reservations, right from the sub-conscious level of his mind even in a pretended role of hostility. This is perhaps the reason why he did much of it and surely overreached the stipulated limit of Krishna's instruction. He not only repeated his disrespectful address of 'you fellow' from time to time but extended the story of allegations unusually long and in the process unconsciously unburdened his mind of a long-standing preoccupation. He accused Yudhisthira of his cowardice quite evident in his flight from the field to seek shelter in a safe place at least two miles away from the place of action. He grieved *inter alia* 'you fellow, I am doing your pleasure with my children, wife and my own life, yet you kill me with the dart of your cruel words. We have no hope of happiness from you. To the utter slight of me you were free with Draupadi, while I was busy killing war-lords for your sake.'

Yate hi nityang taba kartumistang
Dāraih sutai jībitenatmana cha,
Ebang yanmāng bāgvishikhena hangsi
Tvattah sukhang na bayang bidmah kingchit.
Māng mābasangsthā droupaditalpa sangstho
Mahārathān pratihanmi tvadarthe.

(Ibid., Chap. 70, 13-14)

"Not only that your unrestrained interest in the game of dice has brought all this misery to us and to all. Sahadeva related all the evils of dice-playing, yet you were not restrained." Arjuna poured venoms of this sort, practically all snatches of his half-conscious or unconscious prepossessions the central point of which must have been Yudhisthira's decision over his already won lady Draupadi, even the game of dice which led to the savage outrage upon that beloved lady may have been a covert reference to that incident. It was Yudhisthira who had surely done grievous wrong with regard to Draupadi by his decision to share her with Arjuna who had won her. This wrong and impious decision was followed by Yudhisthira's even greater crime to stake the lady in a game of dice when he had nothing else left to lose, his love of game made him completely blind to all the implications of sin in an addiction like this. All these must have been unsettling secretly the depths of Arjuna's mind, when he cannot be considered as a block of wood or stone. All these came out in his even simulated orgy of anger and gave vent to its pent up force. Surely Krishna did not teach him to do it, yet he did.

Arjuna unconsciously lapsed into real anger and gave vent to his injured feelings, which actually got the better of his sense. So when he came to his senses, which he was sure to do at the partial release of his secret obsession by this means, he felt extremely ashamed and in the opposite reaction unsheathed his sword to kill himself. It is an unexpected evolution, although not unpsychological. Lord Krishna once more met it by an ethical formulation as he did on another similar occasion. He asked Arjuna to kill himself spiritually as he did with regard to his respected elder brother by self-praise. Self-praise is considered self-immolation in scripture. Krishna enjoined it because self-killing is a greater sin than murder, even the murder of a brother. Any way this should be avoided, that can be better done by reviving self-consciousness. Krishna perhaps took that psychology as a remedial course for Arjuna. Arjuna listened to him and thought it to be a satisfactory alternative. He started searching into all his merits, the life work of a hero, which must have at once effected a thorough change of his mood. Krishna wanted only that.

Arjuna was relieved, after all he did not want to destory himself, wanted only a way out of that double disgrace, Krishna offered him an opportunity. He immediately took it and did it over much, which surely was not Krishna's meaning. He started self-praise and extended it to a limit which Yudhisthira may have wished. Arjuna had none for his match in this world except Mahadeva whose blessing had graced him. He would presently kill Karna in that terrible chariot under Lord Krishna's steersmanship. And finally bowed to the elder brother saying, "You will understand at last why I behaved so."

Yudhisthira's reaction was immediate and very sharp. He acknowledged in his grief all the charges brought against him. Yes, he did much evil which led to their misfortune; really he was indulging in sins and pleasures of the flesh, he must expiate all these follies with his life, he eventually asked Arjuna to chop off his head, which he rightly deserved, or else he must renounce this world for the forest to leave them in peace and prosperity. Now at this stage Lord Krishna came to explain the whole episode, why Arjuna drew his sword and addressed reproachful and flippant words to Yudhisthira. Disrespect to superiors is equivalent to their death. With these words of appeasement Krishna begged leave to withdraw to meet the challenge of Karna whom the eldest Pandava could then count among the dead.

Yudhisthira, on his part, acknowledged in clear terms

Krishna's crucial role in this confusion which, he believed, could lead to the most disastrous misfortune, for their not knowing true Dharma. They were both at their wit's end, and steeped in ignorance. Practically to outside observers they were under their personal obsession which beclouded their clear vision, their religion was a religion of obsession.

Krishna knew it, the clear eyed Lord of the world must lord it over with that highest aid of human competence; when in his human form he will do everything in a human way, drawing upon nothing extra-terrestrial. Krishna now saw that Arjuna had already overshot the true measure of necessity in his use of reproach, he had added an extra dose of his own reserved wrath. So Krishna asked Arjuna to beg his elder brother's forgiveness before he started for the field. The whole scene of fraternal endearment has all been enacted under the stewardship of Lord Krishna. Practically he righted the wrongs both the brothers did in their misconception of Dharma, really mixed up with their undetected complexes. Their reconciliation and affectionate embrace before the eyes of Krishna proved an even tenderer scene with tears and sighs from both the sides. After that outburst of sentiments was over Yudhisthira described his distress at the onslaught of Karna and his extreme physical torments at his hand. He explained to Arjuna why he went to hysterics of abuse of this kind. What he wanted was actually a just retaliation for this despicable defeat. So he vowed once more to take his own life in case they failed to despatch Karna.

Yudhisthira is swayed by his impulses as Arjuna too is, even their sense of Dharma and truth is coloured by their undetected passions and reservations. But Krishna in his human role is never coloured by any such complexes, he demonstrates the state of the highest attainable tranquillity, in Indian version Mukti, by his well-principled adaptability, adaptability to one particular achievement of life and its acceleration for one and all. He could not allow Arjuna to kill his brother for the sake of a pledge, also a braggadocio sort of complex, nor could see him destroy his own life for the shame of his extravagant reproach, again out of suppressed wrath in the past. Neither of them fulfils the purpose of life, nor does it contribute to the furtherance of its true object.

Krishna revealed the other side of Dharma, preservation of life and its acceleration is what Dharma stipulates, but why then this wide preparation for the killing of Karna and his cohort ? Krishna did not leave it vague. He talked to Arjuna the whole ethics of this killing while driving his chariot to the battlefield. Not all killing is unethical, that is the mystery of it, which even the greatest interpreter of ethics may fail to discern, Krishna earlier told Arjuna. Krishna knew all the merits of Karna, he recounted how great a hero he was, even Arjuna was not a match for his strength, he was almost an invincible enemy. But his one great defect was his constant support of Duryadhana, the side of sin and crime, which over-poised all his good qualities. He turned to a nurturing force of evil, so even greater in effect than evil *per se.* He had always been on the side of the evil-doers, the Kauravas, and against the Pandavas. And among his misdeeds were his stewardship in the tricky game of dice, in which the Pandavas had to lose all and even to stake their wife, and also his leering grimace while Draupadi was being disrobed in the Kaurava court, and his open taunt towards her :

Binastāh Pāndabāh Krishne shāshvatang narakang gatāh.
Patimanyang Prithushroni brinisva mridubhāsini

* * * * * *

Dāsbhāryā cha Pānchāli svayang dāsi cha shobhane.
(Ibid., Chap. 73, 83-86)

The Pandavas have all perished and gone to eternal hell, hence take another husband, Oh, well-buttocked soft-voiced Krishna, thou art spoused to slaves, and now herself turned one—thus Karna mocked her.

The severity of Karna's role in the whole of the Kurukshetra drama is so acutely painted by Lord Krishna that Arjuna quite understood how dangerous he was not only as a personal enemy but as a constant source of evil. Evil with added power of destruction and corruption must not be ignored or left alone to grow in strength, but ought to be eradicated root and branch for the safety and security of life itself : not to do it is to go against

Dharma, because it is tantamount to a tacit crusade against life. Krishna proclaimed this secret of Dharma to Arjuna drawing only some exciting misdeeds of the giant. He ended by saying that Karna could in no way be spared to do proper justice to the ethics of life. This will never soil his sense of religion, but rather establish it upon a firmer basis.

INDEX